NETWORK MARKETING ONLINE

The Complete Guide to MLM – How to Create A Passive Income Stream and Realize your Dreams by Working from Home with Social Media

ELETTRA MORO

© Copyright 2019 by Elettra Moro
All rights reserved.

This document is geared towards providing exact and reliable information with regards to the topic and issue covered. The publication is sold with the idea that the publisher is not required to render accounting, officially permitted, or otherwise, qualified services. If advice is necessary, legal or professional, a practiced individual in the profession should be ordered.

- From a Declaration of Principles which was accepted and approved equally by a Committee of the American Bar Association and a Committee of Publishers and Associations.

In no way is it legal to reproduce, duplicate, or transmit any part of this document in either electronic means or in printed format. Recording of this publication is strictly prohibited and any storage of this document is not allowed unless with written permission from the publisher. All rights reserved.

The information provided herein is stated to be truthful and consistent, in that any liability, in terms of inattention or otherwise, by any usage or abuse of any policies, processes, or directions contained within is the solitary and utter responsibility of the recipient reader. Under no circumstances will any legal responsibility or blame be held against the publisher for any reparation, damages, or monetary loss due to the information herein, either directly or indirectly.

Respective authors own all copyrights not held by the publisher.

The information herein is offered for informational purposes solely, and is universal as so. The presentation of the information is without contract or any type of guarantee assurance.

The trademarks that are used are without any consent, and the publication of the trademark is without permission or backing by the trademark owner. All trademarks and brands within this book are for clarifying purposes only and are the owned by the owners themselves, not affiliated with this document

Table Of Contents

INTRODUCTION 1

   The Advantages and Disadvantages of Network Marketing 6

   Extraordinary Considerations 7

CHAPTER ONE: NETWORK MARKETING ONLINE 8

   The Internet and Network Marketing ... 12

   Maintaining a Successful Multilevel Marketing Business 17

   The Right Way to Recruit People to Sell For You 19

CAHPTER TWO: MULTI-LEVEL MARKETING (MLM) 25

   Introducing Multi-Level Marketing 25

   Preparing to Start Your MLM Business 29

   Understanding the Basis of Your MLM Business 34

   Dealing with the Hardest Parts of MLM Routines 35

   Understanding What It Takes In Sponsoring 36

Questions to Ask Before Becoming Involved In an Online MLM Business .. 43

What is MLM? 44

Is MLM Legal? 44

CHAPTER THREE: MAKING YOUR PROFILE TO BE ATTRACTIVE 53

What MLMS Wants to Do for Network Marketing Distributors 53

Tips to Creating a MLM Attractive Profile 57

CHAPTER FOUR: THE TYPES OF SOCIAL MEDIA POSTS YOU SHOULD BE FOCUSING ON 79

Sixteen Social Media Etiquette for MLM: The DOs 89

DON'Ts on Social Media in MLM 98

CHAPTER FIVE: USING SOCIAL MEDIA TO FIND PROSPECTS 122

MLM Success Tips: What you Need When Joining a Network Marketing Business 129

CHAPTER SIX: HOW TO REACH OUT TO SOMEONE ON SOCIAL MEDIA 149

Steps to a "Master Style" Online MLM Business... 154

WORDS TO USE 165

Utilizing the Internet to Explode Your MLM Marketing Business 170

Online MLM - How to Avoid Stressing Out.. 176

Ways to Avoid Stress in Online MLM 178

Powerful MLM Recruiting Must Involve Multiple Steps 192

CHAPTER SEVEN: HOW TO PRESENT YOUR PRODUCT 197

Best Simple Ways to Sell your MLM Products.. 197

How Attraction Marketing Works 197

Marketing a MLM Product 202

Keys to MLM Attraction Marketing... 205

CHAPTER EIGHT: FOLLOW UP WITH YOUR PROSPECTS 213

What Is Follow-Up? 213

Why Follow Up? 214

Top deals tips for the development 223

Complete Project Planning Sets You Off On the Right Track 224

Restoring Prospects Who Disappear into the Black Hole 228

INTRODUCTION

D**efinition:** Network Marketing is a form of business in which a merchant network is required to assemble the business. Typically, such businesses are additionally multilevel marketing in nature in that payouts happen at more than a level.

Network marketing is a business model that relies upon individual to-individual deals by autonomous agents, frequently telecommuting from home.

There are numerous trustworthy network marketing activities, yet some have been reviled as fraudulent business models. Network marketing is a sort of business opportunity that is prominent with individuals searching for low maintenance, adaptable businesses. Network marketing projects highlight a low forthright venture - typically just a couple of measure of cash for the buy of an item test pack - and the chance to sell a product offering straightforwardly to companion, family and other individual contacts. Most network marketing programs additionally request that members enroll different deals delegates. The volunteers establish a rep's "downline," and their deals create salary for those above them in the program.

At the point when individuals purchase their products and ventures from you, you get commissions on deals. There are various things that you can sell, from toiletries, for example, shampoos, cleansers, and body washes; to even website servers and web space online. Multi-level marketing can enable you to make a ton of companions, if just based on having individuals purchase from you. In this phase of multi-level marketing, you should put your sales rep's cap on and begin talking like a sales rep: you can't be a hard selling sales rep, yet neither would you be able to be excessively negligent in your selling.

On the off chance that you are searching for individuals to whom you can sell your merchandise and ventures, at that point you may need to know the intricate details of your objective market? You should realize the age gathering to which you are providing food, and from that point derive where this age gathering hangs out online, what this age gathering needs, what this age group is most worried about, and how much this age group is happy to pay for specific products and administrations.

Along these lines, you can all the more likely design your marketing proclamation and you can connect with your objective market quicker, state by posting on message sheets and connecting to online journals.

Another route for you to profit from multi-level marketing is through referrals. In multi-level marketing, you can allude somebody to the program, and each time that individual profits, you get your own bonuses as well? This implies you don't just need to enroll countless individuals to fill in as your "downlines" in multi-level marketing. You additionally need to enlist individuals who are as driven as you seem to be, and are as eager to invest energy, cash, and exertion so as to get their own downlines, sell their merchandise and ventures, and, to put it plainly, be as energetic in the business as you may be.

How might you best do this? To enroll individuals don't make a one in million guess and don't spam people groups' post boxes with messages on how they should join your program? Converse with individuals each one in turn, and construct your downlines through quality, not amount.

These are just a couple of parts of multi-level marketing that you might need to observe as you begin chipping away at your new online business. For more data, converse with individuals who have officially experienced multi-level marketing, and who have profited through their MLM attempts. You may likewise need to do some exploration all alone, state by counseling marketing and deals books, so as to all the more likely style your marketing articulation. Whwn you can sell well, and sell the possibility of MLM well without seeming like you are pushing individuals into a business, at that point you can make cash off this business model.

Network marketing is known by an assortment of names, including multilevel marketing, cell marketing, associate marketing, purchaser direct marketing, referral marketing, or locally established business diversifying.

Organizations that pursue the network marketing model regularly make levels of sales reps—that is, sales reps are urged to select their very own networks of salesmen. The makers of another level (or "upline") procure commission without anyone else deals and on deals made by the individuals in the level they made (the "downline"). In time, another level can grow one more level, which contributes more commission to the individual in the top level just as the center level.

In this manner, the income of salesmen rely upon enrollment just as item deals. The individuals who got in ahead of schedule and are in a top level make the most.

The Advantages and Disadvantages of Network Marketing

There is some disgrace connected to networking marketing, particularly those with multiple levels, which can be described as fraudulent business models—that is, the sales reps in the top level can make amazing measures of cash on commissions from the levels underneath them. The individuals on the lower levels will procure substantially less. The organization makes cash by selling costly starter packs to newcomers.

The intrigue of network marketing is that a person with a ton of vitality and great deals abilities can make a productive business with an unobtrusive venture.

A decent dependable guideline, as per the Federal Trade Commission (FCC), is that solitary level network marketing activities will in general be more trustworthy than multi-level plans, in which individuals make cash dependent on the quantity of merchants they select.

Extraordinary Considerations

Anybody considering joining a network marketing activity ought to do their exploration before settling on a choice. Think about these inquiries:

- Was it pitched as an opportunity to make cash by selling products or by enrolling others?
- What is the reputation of the organization's authors?
- Are you actually excited about the products?
- Are individuals you know energetic about the products?
- Is the item being advanced adequately?
- Do you predict a generally quick pathway to benefits or very distant stepping water?

CHAPTER ONE

NETWORK MARKETING ONLINE

The basic essence of network marketing is building networks of individuals who purchase and sell products. What better spot to construct a network of individuals than on a definitive overall network- - the web? As per Internet World Stats, starting at 2006, there were more than 1 billion individuals online around the world. It's no big surprise that the web is the spot to go to construct a network marketing business.

The advantages to building your business online are broad - you can work in shorts and a T-shirt, you just converse with individuals who are profoundly intrigued, your business is working for you day in and day out, your support expenses are low, and it's anything but difficult to extend universally. Most significant, anybody can do it- - you don't need to be a PC virtuoso to discover achievement.

Your initial step is to make an online nearness. Before you start assembling a site, you need a space name. You could verify your own character site (yourname.com), which is constantly a smart thought. Another methodology is to pick an area that identifies with the name of your network marketing gathering or group, for example, wealthteam.com or prosperitygroup.com. Or then again you may need a space that says something fascinating, for example, increaseyourwealth.com or massiveincome.com. Think of a lot of thoughts, at that point check your decisions on a vault site until you discover one that is accessible.

When you have a space, you'll have to purchase facilitating administrations and after that start to fabricate your site. In the event that you don't have a clue how to plan a site, you can either contract a planner or utilize a site developer that offers pre-made layouts through your host. Regardless of which technique you pick, your site ought to incorporate the accompanying:

- Information about your organization, item and opportunity

- A framework for requesting your item or enrolling to work a business
- Information about preparing and your help group
- A rundown of the upsides of joining your organization and group
- The offer of a free digital book, archive or bulletin if clients give you their name and a legitimate email
- An automated assistant that sends follow-up messages to everybody who gives their contact data. Ensure it can likewise convey bulletins.

When you have your site ready for action, you have to begin marketing it. I prescribe utilizing two to five diverse marketing strategies and staying with them for in any event a couple of months before reexamining them. Marketing strategies you might need to give a shot include:

- Free classifieds
- Pay-per-click promoting
- Paid pennant promoting

- Writing articles that incorporate connections to your website
- Starting a blog
- Participating in discussions and newsgroups
- Starting an email pamphlet

Every one of these techniques will help make introduction and pull in prospects, however my preferred marketing strategy is "attraction marketing." Any time you can build up yourself as a specialist, you'll draw in individuals keen on the theme you know about. Make sure to incorporate articles or digital books on your site that set you up as a specialist.

As you draw in prospects, you'll need a database to monitor them. Viewpoint has an extraordinary contact director, however in the event that you make something all alone, ensure it has enough space to monitor a prospect's name, email, telephone number and address, and has a territory where you can compose remarks.

When a prospect is in your database, send them an individual email to check whether they found the data on your site to be important and to decide their level of enthusiasm for your business. Use messages to make an affinity with the prospect and push them toward a telephone call. On the off chance that you have a powerful web introduction and follow-up framework and a prospect consents to talk with you by telephone, there's a decent shot that individual will join your business or buy your item.

The keys to network marketing online are a strong nearness, consistency and perseverance, so get out there and assemble your framework, and stick with it until it creates the outcomes you look for.

The Internet and Network Marketing

Today web – network marketing is detonating. 10 years back, many people are being acquainted with network or Multilevel marketing where presented by a companion or relative, somebody that you trusted, today it's simply not the situation.

Through the web, we can bring our network marketing openings and products to a huge number of individuals around the world. Before, we were constrained to static websites, discussions, visit rooms, and moment errand person.

Today we have, web journals, Twitter, Facebook, and so on… just to give some examples, or Web 2.0 in the event that you favor that antique.

Today we can bring or prospects moment sound, video and full clarifications of our business in a flash, yet even with this given by numerous individuals of the network marketing organizations, most wholesalers don't have a clue how to use this viably.

Today, I may really need to concur with them on this issue, tying the web and network marketing together requires something beyond the capacity to get a site online. The subject simply like some other, requires implicit information, something that not many can instruct you!

Actually, the vast majority will surrender well before any quantifiable outcomes originate from it. So they go to the easy routes of driving traffic by means of social media strategies, and still don't comprehend why they have poor outcomes. On the off chance that you are attempting to tie the web and network marketing together what do you need?

1.) Tacit Knowledge.

2.) A Domain Name.

When choosing a space name, it used to be critical to choose a name with keywords in it. This has turned out to be almost inconceivable today. In any case, we see websites that don't have watchwords stuffed into their space name improving internet searcher rankings.

When you're serious about your business, and think you'll stick around in network marketing for quite a while, I'd suggest that you get your name if at all conceivable. Get your name regardless of whether you don't anticipate utilizing it for some time!

3.) Web Hosting.

With regards to web facilitating, we're all searching for deals, recollect that we frequently get what we pay for. Everybody ought to have an individual site, this tells your clients and prospects exactly what your identity is.

You can discover facilitating in an assortment of spots, regularly they will have programming as a major aspect of the facilitating to construct basic websites. One source prescribed even gives you FREE web facilitating as a major aspect of its membership administration. A presentation page as well as a total, proficient evaluation, and content administration arrangement.

4.) Web Design Software.

By and large you'll require programming so as to structure and work with your sites, front page and so forth. There are different variant of website architecture programming out there, however the vast majority will utilize one of the two recorded previously.

I realize everybody likes to do things inexpensively however don't utilize free formats, you can spend less than one hundred dollars and get an extraordinary layout for you site.

5.) Auto-responder System.

Remaining in contact with your prospects is fundamental in today's commercial center. Organizations both enormous and little utilize email marketing to arrive at their objective market.

6.) The ability and assurance to tie the web and network marketing together!

Building a site can be both disappointing and elating simultaneously. There is a considerable number of assets and books out there regarding the matter including the manuals that accompany the product.

You don't require Expensive SEO Software!

These activities are however venturing stones!

The main way you can arrive is by conversing with enough prospects and genuinely focusing. You need to apply what you've perused, tuned in to, into down to earth application…

On the off chance that you're not kidding about structuring your web network marketing business, at that point possibly you need the resources that can help you the most.

Maintaining a Successful Multilevel Marketing Business

Network marketing's business model is just utilizing the intensity of coordinated connections to showcase and appropriate products to buyers. Network marketing organizations engage autonomous business visionaries to adapt to the most popular type of marketing, which is informal marketing. A network marketing proficient is somebody who use their social and expert connections to market, sell and circulate products or administrations. Simultaneously, the person will likewise be building a group of other people who do likewise.

Network Marketing resembles a pyramid, where the individual at the top profits. A decent network marketing organization rewards administration, much the same as any organized business. Most businesses have a pyramid structure where the individuals at the top, i.e. Chiefs, SVPs, VPs, are the most generously compensated individuals in the organization. The one of a kind open door you have with a Network Marketing business is that you START at the highest point of your business, and your pay will be subject to how enormous is a group you work "beneath" you.

"You need to join a ground floor organization to profit."

This is a sustained fantasy utilized by network advertisers who fabricate impact, and hop from organization to organization, and influence this legend to enroll individuals from other Network Marketing organizations. No network marketing organization has ever "soaked" a market; it's only an impression of "immersion," not a reality.

Besides, you need to know many individuals, or be great at deals to be fruitful. Numerous great network marketing organizations give a framework and preparing, so paying little respect to the size of your network – or capacity to sell, you can be fruitful. Everything else is a learnable ability, and you have a plenitude of individuals to work on networking with.

You have to concentrate on helping other people to get what they need, and you will get what you need.

K.I.S.S. – Keep It Super Simple!

Also, recall, everything will rise and fall on LEADERSHIP!

The Right Way to Recruit People to Sell For You

First: Invite individuals to take a gander at your business suggestion with an immediate or circuitous methodology. An immediate methodology is requested that they take a gander at your business for themselves. A roundabout methodology is requesting that somebody take a gander at your business to help you with suggestions or referrals. There are a wide range of examples of language that you can utilize dependent on the relationship you have with the prospective enlist. The welcome procedure is a significant expertise to learn. Your welcome has a great deal to do with whether the individual will join your group or bolster your business.

Second: Most individuals don't join on the primary presentation, so fortune lies in the subsequent procedure. You should propel the prospective enlisted people comprehension of your business on each subsequent communication. Concentrate on structure as a more grounded compatibility and relationship en route.

Third: Use outsider social verification to approve the chance and to build the prospect's conviction that somebody like them can be effective with your organization.

Fourth: Do a course of action meet and get the individual off to a quick begin. How you begin another individual has a ton to do with their dedication level and to what extent they will fabricate the business. Since network marketing is a deliberate business, the maintenance of merchants is a significant expertise to learn.

Fifth: Create a triumphant situation for your group to develop and for them to bolster off the vitality and energy of others.

Obviously the organization needs an item that makes a substantial interest in the commercial center. In the event that that is the situation, you influence your network, and networks of others, to increase a crowd of people of at least one. Offer the advantages of your products or administrations, and offer stories. Stories sell and realities tell.

By and large, a roundabout methodology is best for loved ones. Request that they bolster your business and vision by basically resolving to investigate what you are doing and why you are doing it. Make it simple for them to state no and remain your companion. Try not to weight anybody. Try not to end up bizarre. Individuals join some network marketing businesses and get so energized that they don't separate their business from their own lives. Try not to divert each discussion with your companions to attempt to enroll them into your business and don't transform your social media pages into a publicizing release board.

The key for progress is to work by a schedule. Plan the occasions you will work your business. Most Network Marketing organizations have apparatuses and occasions framework that enable you to use your time by elevating the SYSTEM to do the lifting.

It's imperative to return to the reasons why you began the business. It's additionally imperative to focus on self-awareness by tuning in and perusing motivating sounds and books. The vast majority feel down in view of the negative contemplations of self-question that begin to crawl into their brains. Many individuals miss precisely that it is so essential to make a triumphant situation for your group to develop in. Customary individuals can win in a remarkable domain.

What are the most valuable aptitudes you've used to accomplish the outcomes you have accomplished in your businesses?

- **Influence** – An initiative is impact, that's it and nothing less. Everything rises and falls on authorities, so it's a fundamental characteristic for progress. Impact is likewise used to adequately and powerfully impart the temperance of a decent item or administration, and to get individuals to state YES! We likewise realize that at deals.

- **Skills** – There are sure specialized aptitudes you requirement for whatever industry you are a piece of, so it's imperative to build up those abilities. In spite of the fact that, they are a little part of what your prosperity will be predicated on. You should in the end figure out how to re-appropriate the things that bode well to redistribute, so you can deal with the business versus in the business.

- **Focus** – In the present quick paced society, the capacity to center is turning into an irregularity. Individuals are everywhere, and effectively diverted. Time the board is a legend, since time is now all around overseen into 24 hours per day. Center Management is the test for all of us. Instructions to remain FOCUSED, and WHAT to concentrate on is likewise a point in itself. It has mentorship to help you in this classification.

- **Work Ethic** – The main spot achievement precedes work is in the lexicon. It's critical to develop your resilience for work. On the off chance that you are doing what you adore, you work can turn into your play.

- **Belief** – As a business person, you are a maker. You transform immaterial thoughts into something substantial, and it requires conviction! In addition to the fact that belief affects your physiology, yet it likewise has an environmental influence that makes the universe begin to contrive to that which you accept.

- **Faith** – The great book says, "Faith is the substance of things sought after, and the proof of things not seen." It expects confidence to continue working when the outcomes are not immediate. Enterprise requires confidence – the confidence to accept notwithstanding when it appears as though accepting isn't working.

CAHPTER TWO

MULTI-LEVEL MARKETING (MLM)

Introducing Multi-Level Marketing

Some consider Salesmanship to be a characteristic quality as is Leadership. Some believe Salesmanship to be an Art. At that point there are the individuals who accept that anybody and everybody can be a Salesman with some preparation. Conventional idea of channel deals and hold deals as ideas are contemplated by each marketing and deals understudy.

From the modest beginnings of mother and pop shops to general stores, selling has made some amazing progress. Aside from these business channels we have likewise observed the idea of direct selling and referral selling having created in the course of the last forty to fifty years.

Over the most recent thirty years or so we have seen another new pattern in deals known as Multi-Level Marketing and this has spread over the globe. However, quietly and connected with a huge number of individuals in selling products and gaining conventional pay for themselves.

It isn't back to discover your companions welcoming you home for a casual get-together throughout the end of the week and you end up purchasing the overwhelming Tupperware products for your home. Correspondingly a large number of individuals are purchasing Home products, Personal Care products just as Food supplements and other way of life products through their companions who happen to be a piece of Amway Network. In the event that you have been presented to these sort of exchanges you have been acquainted with what is known as Multi-Level Marketing or Network marketing.

Network marketing is a genuinely new idea that was created in the mid-1980s and has spread the whole way across the globe. Today it includes housewives, corporate officials, resigned people, understudies just as individuals from varying backgrounds occupied with selling through network and early fair wages while they keep on pursuing their occupations.

Network Marketing is another wonder that has made progress over the most recent three decades and thus there isn't quite a bit of research, study and writing that is accessible as in the other conventional speculations and routine with regards to Marketing. The WFDSA - World Federation of Direct Selling Agents have characterized Network selling as "Marketing and Selling of Products and Services straightforwardly to the Consumers in an up close and personal and in spots like home, working environment and different workplaces other than retail deals areas." On the essence of it this definition depicts the Network Marketing in the correct manner. Anyway you will see that this definition can hold notwithstanding for Direct Selling which isn't equivalent to Multi Level or Network selling. There are a few trademark contrasts in the modalities that these two deals techniques pursue however there are similitudes as well.

In the two instances of Direct Selling just as Network marketing, the selling occurs on 'Balanced premise's the place the sales rep comes in eye to eye contact with the client or client. Along these lines both the strategies included the End User or End client toward one side and the Sales individual on the other. In the two cases the Salesman included, assumes the job of affecting the decision makers. The fundamental diverse between the two techniques is to do with the hierarchical arrangement of the business groups just as the strategy for pay and pay age. Anyway hypothetically Network marketing is viewed as a piece of Direct Selling techniques.

Multi-Level Marketing is a movement that anybody can take up anytime of time throughout everyday life and produce salary. There are thousands who take up MLM alongside their principle professions and after that there are such huge numbers of who have turned out to be moguls by occupying MLM on full time premise and making it their prime work. This type of marketing does not require any capability or any speculations. Other than producing pay, the individual gets the opportunity to fabricate social contacts and connections too which is viewed as an additional advantage.

Preparing to Start Your MLM Business

Being youthful and with a developing family means having a 'List of things to get' that is very long. You have your fantasies and the other's in the family have theirs as well. So when a chance to procure additional cash other than your present salary through your calling is positively going resemble a God sent chance. In the event that you have experienced the MLM recommendation that has been displayed to you and inspected the idea altogether, addressed loved ones and taken a choice to feel free to take it up, it plans yourself and approach the business in an expert way so you can make a triumph out of your new pursuit.

- **Characterize your Goals**

    When you have comprehended the idea, what is normal out of you and are agreeable that you can begin your business adventure give at some point for your choice to soak in. Set aside some effort to have an independent perspective or ask yourself about how you will characterize your achievement in the new pursuit. Your prosperity definition relies on what you need to escape this action and how this endeavor will satisfy you.

For certain individuals making a million bucks through the business may be the objective while others may very well be content with a couple of thousand dollars to assist them with their momentary objectives. Other than monetary pay desires, you should likewise take a gander at the other result or impacts of the business and add them to your rundown of accomplishment as well. Multi-Level Marketing (MLM) business is tied in with gathering new individuals, building connections and cooperating. Over the span of your business you will get the chance to meet many individuals who will remain companions with you and in this way your social circle will get extended as well. You will likewise wind up sharpening your aptitudes and improving as a communicator and an expert as well. Thusly it distinguishes your objectives and points and characterize the level of progress that you wish to go for and accomplish through MLM business.

- **Be prepared to Invest**

The facts demonstrate that MLM business adventure does not require any capital venture and as a rule you should purchase only the starter unit costing not exactly a hundred dollars. However, at that point you will be required to contribute your time and exertion reliably to construct your business. This implies you will initially need to take a gander at your expert and individual needs and work out to perceive how much time you will probably take out during the night times and during ends of the week to dedicate to MLM business. This can mean eliminating TV and superfluous items and making changes with your family as well.

Other than setting aside a few minutes, you should almost certainly travel and meet individuals at better places. In this way you should be rationally arranged and have the correct way to have the option to travel.

- **Home Office**

Before you begin with the MLM business, it is smarter to distinguish and prepare with a little office at your home. Working in a committed office condition encourages you get progressively engaged and work proficiently as well. Other than you will require the space to have the option to meet a gathering of individuals, to talk about and make introductions to them as well. You will require fundamental correspondence and office framework to be set up obviously.

Over the span of gathering individuals over the town and far off spots or visit workplaces, you should travel. In this manner until such time that you begin procuring pay from your business exchanges, you should keep some money for costs that you are probably going to cause on voyaging and so on.

- **Accounting and Record Keeping**

One other significant order that you should teach directly before you begin with real business is to begin with money related to planning, accounting and record keeping. It is ideal to have spending plans for various heads of costs worked out ahead of time. When you begin bringing about consumption, ensure that you gather the majority of the bills and solicitations and record for them as well. You should keep up all records and books of records for your assessment forms. It is additionally prudent that you open a different financial balance with the end goal of your MLM business and don't consolidate it with your own record.

With point by point arranging and readiness, you will discover it smoother to begin with your MLM business and work proficiently and expertly. With everything set up, you will have additional time, vitality and regard for commit to building your business.

Understanding the Basis of Your MLM Business

By-passing All the Pitfalls

It is safe to say that you are not kidding about acquiring a living through MLM or Network Marketing business? Out of misinterpretation, disappointment, and terrible encounters in their past MLM adventures a few people may have chosen that MLM is anything but an appropriate route even to acquire a not too bad living, let alone to make it a way to be well off. Some other individuals may have censured MLM and indicated sharp face when drawn closer by their companions who welcomed them to engage in MLM business.

How and where do MLM get its reputation from? It originates from misguided judgment and is allowed by many MLM's failures. A portion of those individuals who disparage MLM and talk awful about MLM may have not in any case attempted any endeavor in MLM business whatsoever. They simply caught wind of something awful or amiss with MLM from MLM and Money Game's failures. Out of numbness, a few people partner all rich-brisk plans, (for example, Money Games, Pyramid Schemes) with MLM or Network Marketing business. This is genuinely a monstrous speculation. These individuals are needing training with the goal that they will discover the genuine nature and attributes of a genuine MLM or Network Marketing business. In the event that you need to get included earnestly in MLM and Network Marketing business and hope to procure better living from it, you need to painstakingly pick the privilege MLM organization. Invest a portion of your energy in directing an exploration about MLM organizations you have considered to engage with. By doing this you will most likely by-pass all traps and genuine impediment that may have bombed numerous individuals who are presently experiencing MLM fear.

Dealing with the Hardest Parts of MLM Routines

There are some basic reasons which cause individuals to avoid MLM business and which are likewise in charge of bombing numerous who, out of curiosity, have attempted to included themselves in a MLM business for quite a while. Numerous individuals figure they will downsize their notoriety and renown when they engage in a MLM business since they envision that their inclusion in MLM will expect them to go entryway to entryway selling products they detest being related with. This sort of individuals absolutely need data and foundation learning about MLM or Network Marketing business. On the off chance that your prospects or hover of colleagues comprise for the most part of this sort of individuals, you will require an increasingly educative methodology in prospecting them. Supply them with great perusers (books, articles, leaflets) about MLM and Network Marketing business. Instruct them first before attempting to support them. Tell them that there are numerous individuals out there who become wildly successful through MLM.

Understanding What It Takes In Sponsoring

To numerous individuals who never carry out a responsibility which requires talking abilities and relational methodology, supporting is a really frightening activity in the first place. For what reason would they say they are terrified of supporting? There must be purposes for this dread. Every individual may have his very own purpose behind dread of supporting. Disconnected supporting includes a long talking exercises which incorporates clarifying, portraying, representing, guaranteeing and trust-building. When you can dissect what you ought to do in supporting, you can set yourself up with the goal that you can perform well in a supporting focused exercises. Considering the segments that make up supporting exercises, you will acknowledge what you have to perform well in supporting. Despite whom you are supporting, it takes a similar dominance of materials and abilities to perform well in supporting. With the dominance of the materials and abilities required close by, you just need to change your strategies and methodologies as per the foundation of an individual you are going to support. Obviously you won't utilize a similar methodology in supporting a senior secondary school graduate as you will in supporting a doctor. In spite of the fact that you utilize similar materials and aptitudes in supporting them.

What materials do you truly need to ace to have the option to perform well in supporting? There are two sorts of materials that you need to ace to perform well in supporting exercises, to be specific:

1. Materials about your MLM organization's profile and the arrangement of remuneration plan and everything identified with this.

2. Materials about the products being promoted by the organization and everything related them. In this way, it is emphatically suggested that when you sign up with any MLM organization, you need to immediately know, in any event general learning about this current organization's profile, its remuneration plan, and the products being promoted.

When you are not keen on getting some answers concerning this, at that point you are not joining the organization to succeed but rather to satisfy your support as well as upline incidentally. You will go no place past being enlisted as a part. This kind of part conceivably makes up the most astounding level of all MLM individuals who will in the long run say, "I am not removed to be a MLM tycoon."

Learning to Handle Rejection Wisely

It is reasonable and human instinct not to promptly acknowledge refusal or dismissal. The vast majority won't take "No" for an answer. Essentially, no one needs to be rejected. In any case, it is likewise the law of nature that there is a "No" to adjust a "Yes", there is a "Light" to adjust a "Dull", and there is a "Decent" to adjust is a "Terrible". In this way, thinking about this law of nature, you should not kill yourself since you are dismissed multiple times today. Some other individuals may have been rejected multiple times today yet resist the urge to panic since they know tomorrow they may get 10 acknowledgments. Such is reality. To these idealistic individuals, life resembles a turning wheel. You will never be on top constantly. What's more, God is of preeminent equity. Succeeding is the privilege of everybody who battles for it. It involves time and constancy.

Duplicating Leaders

For what reason do individuals manufacture a network? There must be a motivation behind why a network is so profoundly respected by the individuals who know the worth of networking. It requires some investment and vitality to construct an enormous network. Building a network is certainly not a one man's work. You will never have an immense network on the off chance that you work alone. It is practically difficult to construct a network alone. The more individuals you need to fabricate a network the simpler and quicker you can set up an immense network. Copying is making an ever increasing number of individuals whose mastery, aptitudes, disposition and activity are like those of their equipped pioneer in connection to their business improvement. On the off chance that one capable pioneer can manufacture a colossal château, much more can be normal from increasingly capable pioneers.

Managing Downlines

The life span of your inflow of lingering and easy revenue lies on your achievement in dealing with your downlines. Your downlines are your advantage, so treat them thusly. Your downline association is an essential foundation of your MLM business. Your business is nothing without your downlines. On the off chance that you bomb in understanding the significance of your downlines, simply envision yourself remaining on a top of a tall structure, at that point all of a sudden comes a major tremor shaking and breaking the establishment and the body of the structure on which you are standing. What is the opportunity of your remaining alive?

Engaging and Rewarding Yourself

Are you felt burnt out on of doing your MLM schedules, being rejected, being disappointed in view of disappointment in accomplishing your very own objective, and in specific cases being abandoned by the individuals whom you used to acquaint with the business. Once more, it is an unavoidable truth that now and again you need to acknowledge the truth of life. Figure out how to acknowledge what you have in your grasp, and what God has conceded to you up until this point. You may have accomplished more than what your partners have, yet you don't understand it or to pompous to state "Much obliged!" to the Creator of this universe.

Attempt to gain from other individuals who have succeeded. Don't simply perceive how rich they are currently, however get familiar with the procedures which they may have imparted to million individuals through their life stories. Did they all of a sudden prevail out of nowhere? You may not understand that you have discovered the correct way to accomplish your long time objectives. Try not to give others a chance to take your fantasies or occupy your heading. Engage yourself when you accomplish some improvement in you MLM profession. Reward yourself for every accomplishment anyway little it might be. Say thanks to "God" for all gift and benevolence conceded to you, at that point you will be guided securely to your goal.

Questions to Ask Before Becoming Involved In an Online MLM Business

Wherever you look on the Internet nowadays, somebody is offering an "incredible new" Internet business opportunity. A large number of these, obviously, are based on MLM models.

A portion of the inquiries posed (or which ought to be asked) by individuals new to MLM and additionally Internet businesses and Internet marketing are:

1. What is a MLM business?
2. Is a MLM business even lawful?
3. Would I be able to profit with a MLM business?
4. Would it be advisable for me to engage with THIS online MLM business?
5. What do I have to do to be fruitful in a MLM business - online or disconnected?

6. Having taken a gander at the things above, do I still REALLY need to do this?

What is MLM?

MLM represents multi-level marketing. Basically, MLM implies that the business enables its merchants or agents to enlist others into a downline. The "selection representative" at that point gathers commissions from deals made by downline individuals just as close to home deals. MLM is normally connected with network marketing which is marketing done basically by listening in on others' conversations.

Is MLM Legal?

MLM itself is an impeccably legitimate route for an organization to disseminate commissions and make an enormous deals power. The issue is that numerous deceitful organizations and people have utilized the MLM model to advance illicit or semi legitimate "products". Ordinarily, the absolute most significant central factor, in spite of the fact that not really the one and only one, in deciding whether a MLM proposition is real is a straightforward inquiry. Is this organization selling an ACTUAL item or administration? Keep in mind; on the grounds that a MLM organization is lawful DOES NOT really imply that it is a decent spot to contribute your time and cash. Get your work done.

Would I Be Able To Make Money With MLM?

Totally. A large number of individuals around the globe are partaking in MLM network marketing adventures and making money. Nonetheless, a MLM opportunity is simply that...an opportunity. There is no assurance that anybody WILL profit with MLM or some other business open door so far as that is concerned. Achievement in any business adventure relies upon a great deal of elements, and for all its evident straightforwardness much of the time, a multi-level marketing business is simply that...a business. Most disappointments in MLM originate from similar reasons that other private companies fall flat; absence of data, absence of instruction about the business, reluctance to act, absence of inspiration, etc.

Is This The Right MLM Business For Me?

The vast majority going into a MLM network marketing business pose one inquiry; "Would i be able to make (parts) of cash with this?" A superior thought is the fit among you and the organization. Not to be chauvinist, however a macho buddy sort of fellow may feel senseless attempting to sell Avon beautifying agents, in spite of the fact that Avon is a tremendous organization with heaps of fruitful male and female delegates. In this model, one may feel progressively great connecting up with an all the more customarily male situated organization.

The best interesting point before bouncing into an association with an organization is your very own preferences. I, for instance, am energetic about wellbeing and wellness, so it is characteristic that I have floated towards those sorts of organizations. The subsequent thought is the way you feel about an individual organization's products or administrations. OK use them yourself? Okay feel great prescribing them to others regardless of whether you were not aligned with the organization?

How Do I Become Successful With An Online MLM Business?

In the disconnected MLM network marketing world, you begin with a decent organization in a field you are enthusiastic about. You get familiar with the item and utilize the item. Try not to attempt to "sell" the item. At that point you sell yourself. You become an important and powerful individual from the network. You expand your network of companions and colleagues. You let it be realized what you do, yet don't compel the item down anyone's throat and don't give an attempt to close the deal except if you are asked to. You DO don't hesitate to offer useful counsel inside your field of mastery, and you should turn into a specialist in your field, and give fair examinations of your positive encounters with the item or administration.

With an online MLM business, the means are basically the equivalent. Your website will typically do a great deal of the selling, however you use discussions, articles, connecting, promotions and web indexes to achieve indistinguishable things from you would do disconnected.

Would I Really Like To Get Involved With An Online MLM Business?

Basically you won't know until you attempt. In any case, beginning a MLM business, or any new business, includes hazard. In the event that you make a plunge with the two feet, quit your place of employment and give it 1000% you may take off to the top or bite the dust. In the event that you cling to your activity for the check, benefits and the social and expert security it gives, you will be constrained in your capacity to develop your business. This does not mean the business WILL NOT develop; it just implies that it will develop all the more gradually. Indeed, even the best business may not develop by a wide margin on the off chance that you can just chip away at it for five to ten hours every week.

By and large, there will be a great deal of self-uncertainty and vulnerability even once the task has started. There will be slacks and moderate movement because of expectations to absorb information, freshness, apprehension, and the failure to work all day on the business. Along these lines, creation of salary, or some other markers of accomplishment, might be bound to happen. In any case, many network advertisers have made incredible progress with the utilization of two basic apparatuses; time and diligence.

MLM Online

MLM preparing that really works? Online MLM insider facts? You got to be messing with me right? On the off chance that there were a wonder such as this, and it really worked, wouldn't you say my upline would've let me know? Things being what they are, the reason has my up line never disclosed to me the super otherworldly mystery? Indeed, odds are they simply don't have the foggiest idea. At times you simply don't have the foggiest idea what you don't have the foggiest idea. That is going to change. It's an ideal opportunity to rip the top of off and uncover a portion of the top online MLM insider facts to the world. Interesting thing, the genuine pioneers give away these insider facts consistently. Folks should simply ask, tragically most never do, including numerous up lines. All in all, what are these mystical online MLM preparing insider facts? How about we make a plunge, look at it, and discover what some are hesitant to uncover.

Online MLM Training Secret - MLM Training isn't Fun

Face it, dismissal sucks. The arrangement of assembling that warm rundown is simply setting you up for agony. All in all, for what reason does customary MLM preparing have you do it? To begin with, it is duplicable and anybody can do it. Second, they need to get you off to a quick begin so you can make a buck and not quit one month from now since you haven't profited. It is extremely ridiculous to feel that you will go out and make oodles of cash in a month or two. However, such huge numbers of individuals expect as well and after that quit when they don't. Fundamentally, the expectation is that from that warm show you get a measly sign up or two and that will spur you to stay with it. There is shrewdness in this, try not to be engaged with anything you wouldn't impart to those nearest too you and building a business is in every case progressively fun on the off chance that you do it with companions. Issue is after the warm rundown is gone despite everything you have to fabricate your business.

Online MLM Training Secret - Turning The Cold Market Warm

MLM preparing people, shockingly, don't invest enough energy in the subject of individual marking. Individual marking is fundamentally situating yourself as a pioneer, the master, somebody who offers an incentive to the MLM prospect. You do this by offering preparing that really works and sharing your own involvement. You may state, "Yet I am not a specialist!" Yes you are. Here is the reason, you definitely comprehend what it feels like to be stuck calling that feared rundown experiencing no after no. You have been there and done that and on the off chance that you ace some straightforward MLM insider facts that really work, at that point you'll have the option to in a general sense change your business. "On the off chance that you manufacture it they will come." has never been more genuine.

It's that straightforward! It's what the specialists do; they brand themselves by helping other people take care of their issues. Online MLM mystery standard number two is bring esteem, assemble trust, and never pitch your organization appropriate out of the door. Help them with their concern first then they will get some information about your chance. So I surmise the last enchantment question is, "How would I become a specialist?" Learn as much as you can about online MLM and through training you will end up being the master in the field. It is this skill that your prospects will be pulled in as well and make them need to tail you.

CHAPTER THREE

MAKING YOUR PROFILE TO BE ATTRACTIVE

MLMS represents Multi-level Marketing Society and it's an association devoted to aiding multi-level marketing wholesalers or advertisers to prevail in their picked field. In the event that you haven't had much karma recently in network marketing, at that point maybe joining MLMS or if nothing else hearing what it brings to the table won't hurt.

What MLMS Wants to Do for Network Marketing Distributors

The MLMS association is committed to advancing altruism among the individuals that make up the multi-level marketing industry. It's an obvious fact to anybody that the MLM business is as yet experiencing the unfavorable impacts of being ceaselessly made a cynosure by the media and the various MLM tricks uncovered throughout the years.

All things considered, if the MLM business has any expectations of structure its notoriety, those lie in the capacity of MLM organizations and merchants to help each other as opposed to devastating one another.

The MLMS association has likewise stepped up to the plate in sorting out occasions of different sorts and purposes for the MLM people group. These occasions are perhaps the most ideal ways for individuals in the MLM business to become acquainted with and gain from one another.

The MLMS has pointed too in giving the best and refreshed assets for the MLM people group to improve their insight and give them the preparation they have to achieve their objectives. Different multi-level marketing openings are additionally offered to MLM advertisers who are simply beginning and may experience considerable difficulties finding the perfect chance to benefit of.

Last however not the least, the MLMS association ensures that it doesn't disregard general society in its targets. It looks to instruct the overall population about reality behind multi-level marketing and ideally right their mixed up impressions about it.

What Do You Get When You Join MLMS?

Joining MLMS is free for a certain thing. You won't need to pay a penny and you unquestionably won't lose anything on the off chance that you register for participation with the Multi-Level Marketing Society. Likewise, there are other fundamental advantages to appreciate from MLMS and these incorporate yet are not restricted to the accompanying:

- **Make Your Own Profile**

    MLMS allows you to promote for nothing. In the Internet, that means a great deal! Not all websites or gatherings will enable you to advance your own products or administrations without anything in return yet MLMS gives you simply that. In your very own profile page, you can tell perusers about what MLM organization you have a place with, the different products, administrations, and openings you're offering to them, and connections to significant websites in your network.

- **Make Your Own Classified Ads**

Once more, this is totally supportive of free! Individuals from MLMS are permitted to make up to ten arranged advertisements in the website's Member Market. These advertisements will be pivoted haphazardly through the MLMS website and showed at the base piece of each page.

- **Advance Your MLM Event**

On the off chance that you have any significant MLM occasion to advance, you can do as such with the Community Calendar at MLMS!

- **Take part in Forums**

At last, you get an opportunity to chat with individuals who really comprehend your worries about MLM on the grounds that they're experiencing very similar things themselves! The MLMS website offers their individuals an opportunity to talk about their issues and ideally discover an answer too in the enrollment discussion.

Tips to Creating a MLM Attractive Profile

#1 Use Your Personal Picture as Your Social Media Profile Picture

Go figure, isn't that so? It says put your image, it doesn't state put your feline, your canine, or even your organization logo! When you're utilizing Social Media to develop your business, individuals need to become more acquainted with you (perhaps snoop on you) and they need to see your grinning face.

#2 Work and Education Section on Social Media – What to do?

Despite the fact that it might entice to go change your boss data to your new Network Marketing organization when you hit submit on your application, if it's not too much trouble trust me when it is said that it won't help you in your business. Why? Since this takes out interest. The objective is to consistently make interest and have individuals asking you "what do you accomplish professionally?" You don't need them Googling the name and building their own judgment.

#3 Stop Selling and Start Story-Telling

Individuals don't go to Social Media to be sold, they're there to be Social. In case you're doing any sort of business on Social Media or you need to, for the love of everything Social, if it's not too much trouble get help on the most proficient method to regard the Social Media stages so you get greater commitment and more individuals getting some information about your business on Social Media.

#4 We're In The Lifestyle Business

Individuals need to carry on with a fun and free life – that is what we're selling. So when you're utilizing Social Media to develop your business, give individuals something great to watch. Post family pictures, post way of life pictures, post about you voyaging and things you're doing. The more you post about way of life and stories, the more your group of spectators develops to know, as, and trust you.

#5 Reach Out To 1-5 People per Day and Leave Them Feeling Good

On Social Media, connect with 1-5 individuals every day and send them a message that makes them feel better. You can leave them a decent remark that truly makes them feel better. I will include, this isn't an ideal opportunity to share any Call to Action or business joins. This is just a message to compliment or leave them feeling great. (Focus on doing this for 30 days, hell – how about we do a Year!) What this does after some time, is it makes a network of individuals that believe you're Awesome and on the off chance that you have a huge amount of individuals who are tailing you and think you Rock, the more individuals that will keen on what it is you're doing.

#6 Do NOT Mention Your Company Name On Social Media (This is the place it gets somewhat questionable)

This is a colossal Social Media Training Tip…

On the off chance that you notice your organization on Social Media, you dispose interest, individuals Google your organization and you free control of the introduction procedure or more regrettable, they may purchase or unite with another person.

Rather, post way of life and tributes and request that individuals connect with you to get familiar with what you have. Which leads me to my next tip…

#7 Ask People to Private Message You

I realize you're presumably inquiring as to whether you aren't posting explicitly about your organization or products, how would you get individuals inspired by what you have?

This is what to do –

In case you're sharing a story, tribute, salary or item example of overcoming adversity, you need to have a Call to Action toward the part of the bargain. This makes interest and leaves your crowd with an incentive without you being salesy or pushing something at them to purchase.

For instance, "In case you're keen on finding out additional, send me a private message. I'd be glad to tell you what we are doing."

#8 Do Not Share Your Company Website Link on Social Media

Like tip #7, we need to share stories and urge individuals to contact us by means of a Private Message for more data. On the off chance that you post your organization website, they'll proceed to Google your organization and you free control of the presentation procedure. You may never at any point realize they were intrigued on the off chance that you share your organization website connect on Social Media.

#9 Social Media Training Tip – Have a Facebook Fan Page!

You could possibly know, yet it is against Facebook's Terms and Conditions to advance any business on your own profile. Many individuals don't have a clue about that, however having a Fan Page gives you moment validity and specialist with your market and more individuals will pay attention to you about your business.

MLM Training: Online MLM, Offline MLM, or Both

MLM is something or other where there is no single method to do it. For instance, with MLM you can work your MLM business online, disconnected, or both.

It's not by chance that I like to work my MLM business online except for some regular postal mail, TV, and paper advertisements (all of which cross-elevate to my online MLM system). Also, one thing I never do is eye to eye prospecting, pitch my own business to companions or family, or call leads.

I for one find online MLM progressively charming, productive, and best of all - robotized. How about we investigate the principle contrast between online MLM versus disconnected MLM.

Discovering MLM Prospects

Disconnected MLM Prospecting - Prospecting can be tedious and for certain individuals - entirely awkward. It can likewise be hard to "sell" your business opportunity or products without a business character or long stretches of understanding. Disconnected MLM is additionally exceptionally hard to target prospects.

Online MLM Prospecting - Requires MLM preparing that spotlights on publicizing and marketing online, however can be adapted rather rapidly. Investigating where prospects visit and putting your MLM before them is likewise simple to learn. Online MLM prospecting does not require deals abilities or a cordial character.

MLM Training

MLM Training Offline - Meetings are at a particular time and place and may not be advantageous for your downline individuals.

Video chats are comparable in that they may not be at a helpful time for everybody.

With offline MLM, people will in general get "beat down" more than online MLM. In this way, ordinary MLM preparing is critical for a gainful downline.

Online MLM Training - With current advancements you can prepare and persuade your downline day by day - at whatever point and any place they may require it. This is an extraordinary advantage that will enable you to keep your group roused and beneficial - even in the midst of shortcoming or wear out.

MLM Duplication

Offline MLM Duplication - Duplication is just conceivable with downline individuals from a similar character types - which is uncommon in this business. Numerous MLM "substantial hitters" will say that it's workable for anybody to just bounce directly in to a framework that is copied effectively. That is simply false.

Online MLM Duplication - Duplication is as simple as the snap of a catch. There is no character prerequisites on the web. MLM online is extremely one of the least demanding marketing frameworks ever on the grounds that there is no requirement for awkward circumstances like eye to eye selling, bringing MLM leads via telephone, or prospecting loved ones. You just arrangement your online MLM framework and it runs like a robot.

Albeit, conventional MLMers once in a while traverse to online techniques, I trust it won't be long until most of MLMers utilize the web for something other than sending MLM prospects to a plain open door diagram website.

On the off chance that you don't as of now utilize the web to prospect, select, train, and rouse your downline online - presently might be on a par with whenever to begin. Despite everything you'll be in front of generally MLMers.

Consider it, the web is up 24 hours out of every day 7 every week. It's a relentless marketing machine. Online MLM lead Generation has been going on now since the web previously arrived. The basic reality is by utilizing the online methodology you can get rid of the people that are not inspired by MLM and center your marketing way to deal with individuals that need to be in your MLM opportunity.

In all honesty there are really individuals online that are hoping to join your MLM opportunity. So as to truly observe accomplishment in MLM nowadays your marketing must incorporate the accompanying...

PPC (pay-per-clicks), article marketing, official statements, websites, ezines, catch pages, deals pages, site improvement, social media, list developers, and so on...

This is the universe of Online MLM Lead Generation, and in the event that you need to be a specialist MLMer and rule your organization, at that point its time you took in your attribute.

The Secret to MLM Business Success Is Having A Good MLM System In Place

The key to MLM business achievement is having a decent MLM framework set up for you and your group to utilize.

You can have the best products and remuneration plan in the business yet in the event that you don't have a decent MLM framework set up you will never accomplish an abnormal state of MLM business achievement. A decent MLM framework should work like a pipe. The majority of our prospects begin as being suspects. You truly don't know whether they will be keen on your item or business. That is the reason it is so imperative to utilize a MLM greeting page as your initial phase in making a decent MLM framework. Suspects that round out the select in structure on your MLM greeting page are then viewed as evident prospects.

The subsequent advance in making a decent MLM framework with the goal that you can have MLM business achievement is to qualify your prospects. Considering your prospects on the telephone and asking them a couple of basic inquiries is the most ideal approach to qualify them. Posing inquiries like "Would you say you are hoping to work low maintenance or full-time from home?", "What amount of cash would you like to make from home?", and my preferred inquiry to pose is "For what reason are hoping to begin a locally established business?" Posing inquiries like these will enable you to make a discussion with your prospect and will enable you to choose whether or not this prospect is able to work with you or not.

The third step in making a decent MLM framework with the goal that you can have MLM business achievement is to send your now qualified prospect to an introduction. The way to making a duplicable MLM framework is to give the devices a chance to take every necessary step for you. All you ought to do is go about as a visit guide taking your certified prospect from presentation to introduction. Most network marketing organizations have both online and disconnected introductions that clarify your products and business plan to your prospects for you so you don't need to do the introductions yourself. It is significant that you have in your mind what the following introduction is that you will send your prospect to. Perhaps the primary introduction is a basic two moment video or sizzle line message that you have your certified prospect watch or tune in to. The second introduction possibly a more extended online video or a disconnected neighborhood meeting.

The forward advance in making a decent MLM framework with the goal that you can have MLM business achievement is to select your prospect. The most ideal approach to enlist your prospect is to take them to your organization's duplicating website and demonstrate to them the diverse starter packs that are accessible. The key inquiry to pose to them is "Which pack might you want to begin with?" Once more, the website ought to do all the clarifying on what is in each pack and what the focal points are to purchasing the bigger packs.

All things being equal, the key to accomplishing an abnormal state of MLM business achievement is having a decent MLM framework set up for you and your group to utilize. A decent MLM framework comprises of having a decent MLM greeting page, a great passing telephone content, great online and disconnected introductions accessible and a decent website to send your prospects to so they can without much of a stretch choose which starter pack is best for them.

The First Essential Steps for Assuring Eventual MLM Success

Most people who don't make MLM progress inadvertently set themselves up for disappointment during the main month or so in business. Here are some basic advances you should methodicallly finish at an opportune time.

MLM Success Step #1: Associate with a demonstrated MLM program.

Such a significant number of people simply join on the grounds that the pretty post card made brilliant guarantees of fast achievement. You should look into the MLM - this is one of the most essential of the MLM privileged insights you should learn. Find it on the web. Peruse an assortment of articles about it. Gauge the upsides and downsides. At the point when conceivable converse with a part who won't be your up-line support and get his appraisal and recommendations. On the off chance that you are new to MLM, never join any MLM that has not officially substantiated itself.

MLM Success Step #2: Estimate the required money related venture before pay starts streaming to you.

Some MLMs require customary buys from all individuals. What amount of will you need to spend before you can reasonably hope to make enough pay to balance that? As MLM privileged insights go, this is one of the most significant - don't focus on overspending forthright.

MLM Success Step #3: Determine the required time speculation.

There are at any rate three sorts of time speculation for you to consider. The first has to do with how much time it will take to truly figure out how to make the framework work. Here's one more of the MLM insider facts: never hold back on your underlying MLM preparing. Without it you will fall flat. Second, is the time it will take to do the selecting of new individuals? Figure out how it will be done and comprehend the sensible course of events. Third, know how much time you should spend doing preparing and supporting your newcomers. It very well may be extensive. Numerous new MLM members come up short in light of the fact that the measure of time required to make MLM progress is simply additional time than they can cut out of their other everyday responsibilities.

MLM Success Step #4: Become educated about multilevel marketing in a general sense.

In addition to the fact that it is basic to know your very own MLM all around, yet you have to learn the same number of general MLM privileged insights as you can. Invest some energy consistently perusing web articles on themes that will help round out your general MLM instruction. Become familiar with the fundamental methods and standards. The more you know the better your opportunity of making MLM progress. On the off chance that it appears to be hard to do only it, consider putting in a couple of bucks and going along with one of the fine MLM preparing programs you can discover on the web.

The Boy Scouts have it right: Be Prepared! They won't wander into the profound dull woods without inclining early how to utilize a compass and how to live off the land if that ought to end up fundamental. Become arranged in multilevel marketing by learning MLM mysteries early and acing the MLM privileged insights you find en route. Hope to become both from your triumphs and from your disappointments. At the start of your MLM experience, don't hope to prevail with each and every thing you attempt. Do hope to gain well from both what works and what doesn't.

To reword the scouts: Be set up to take in significant exercises from both your triumphs and your non victories.

Wrong Reasons to Join MLM Type Business Models

Network Marketing or "MLM" perhaps a phenomenal strategy to acquire everything from a modest extra salary to copious full time living. In any case, numerous individuals need to join MLM type openings without really getting a handle on what they're getting themselves associated with. This is maybe perhaps the best reason a few people have too much misguided musings in regard to this kind of business model. MLM functions admirably on the off chance that you do it well...end of story.

So, here are six wrong reasons to join MLM:

1) Making "pain free income"- MLM organizations are quite proficient at displaying their organization as a basic 1-2-3 strategy that everyone can do and be changed into a moment tycoon, particularly online. It's practically normal to bring into play out and out misrepresented direct mail advertisements. This resembles asserting that anyone who can open a jar of corned meat could be an ace culinary specialist. Try not to misunderstand me, I do accept a lot of individuals CAN flourish in MLM in the event that they get into the correct mentality. However, you should be set up to learn numerous things and you WILL need to work!

2) Desiring to join MLM and aimlessly accepting that an item is so radiant it will sell itself- This is an agent error, considering most MLM frameworks simply aren't exclusively about the item. In MLM, it won't make any difference on the off chance that you are selling a propelled item that contains each mineral and nutrient under the sun on the off chance that you don't get a handle on what network marketing is extremely about. On the off chance that you want to join MLM for the item consider your marketing at first. In any case the item, marketing starts things out.

3) Hunting an inappropriate prospects. We've all accomplished it - you call a natural amigo you haven't stayed in contact with for quite a long time and you need to orchestrate a gathering concerning "something you will reveal to him increasingly about when you get together." I'm not saying that your companion couldn't be a possibly qualified MLM prospect. Be that as it may, in a great deal of cases, calling every one of your companions is a dreadfully awkward approach to do MLM, particularly in the event that they don't have a business disapproved of mindset. That is the place about all individuals needing to join MLM miss the point.

4) Earning huge amounts of money in a fast timeframe. Nearly all MLM tribute appear to go something like this: "In my first month I picked up $800!" Although not totally lies, tributes like these are collected from people who chose to join MLM toward the starting phases of the organization. More often than not, MLM openings have an actual existence cycle that develops energetically to start with. Now of unstable advancement it very well may be simple as pie to get many included individuals day by day, with similarly little exertion. On the off chance that you join MLM after this, it is significantly progressively hard to see moment results and it requires more noteworthy exertion to draw in new individuals into the organization. Quality and assurance will be expected to prevail now.

5) Top Guru embraces this MLM program- They've earned a huge number of dollars with this chance and they're aren't bashful telling everybody how simple it was for them. They're most likely not lying either.

It wasn't difficult...for them. Taking into account how they definitely realize all the perfect individuals. Additionally, they have the advantages: immense email records, front line Internet marketing apparatuses to successfully market to countless individuals. In the event that you are genuinely new to this game, it is a perilous plan to accept that you could rapidly perform accomplishments like a network marketing master. OK contrast your hitting the fairway aptitudes with that of Tiger Woods? In the event that you need to join MLM and be proficient, get familiar with the abilities to market to thousands preceding turning into a master.

6) Thinking this will be a free business to oversee - Many individuals erroneously envision that they can advertise solely with the expectation of complimentary utilizing the Internet. In spite of the fact that the facts confirm that there are a couple of satisfactory minimal effort Internet marketing strategies you can utilize, you ought to never trick yourself into expecting that Internet marketing will be a no cost undertaking. In like manner, the online game is in many cases genuinely furious and it costs time and money to gain proficiency with the aptitudes to advertise your chance online.

MLM can be an energizing method to profit yet your motivation to join MLM shouldn't be founded on the misguided judgments talked about above. The individuals who neglect to understand this are damned.

CHAPTER FOUR

THE TYPES OF SOCIAL MEDIA POSTS YOU SHOULD BE FOCUSING ON

The MLM can be a very tricky business. In the event that the cards are played right, at that point you can win millions by nearly sitting idle. There are numerous ways that you can make progress in MLM business. There are numerous MLM achievement tips that you may discover helpful to develop your business. These MLM achievement tips are needed by all organizations that are going to begin a MLM organization. These MLM achievement tips will assist you with making your organization prosper after some time.

There are many preparing projects and organizations that spend significant time in giving out these MLM achievement tips. In the event that you are a newcomer to the business, at that point you ought to go to these instructional meetings so you can get some great MLM achievement tips. Outfitted with these MLM achievement tips you can likewise develop your business the manner in which you need it to and simultaneously be effective. These MLM achievement tips are for the most part offered by experienced MLM business individuals.

There are numerous classes held that offer MLM achievement tips to individuals who are happy to learn. These MLM achievement tips have advanced over long stretches of statistical surveying and improvement. These MLM achievement tips will assist you with getting the best out your market and build up the best drives that you have in your grip. The MLM achievement tips will without a doubt see to your accomplishment in your business adventure. You can develop your MLM framework around these MLM achievement tips. These MLM achievement tips can likewise be gathered online on the web also.

The MLM achievement tips that are accessible on the web are essential. The most fundamental factor to have accomplishment in a MLM business or the most essential MLM achievement tips is to have great correspondence. On the off chance that you are a wholesaler or a vender of an item, at that point you ought to have the option to sell and market your item to other people. In the event that you for instance sell speakers, at that point you ought to have the option to persuade your clients why they should purchase just your speakers. They ought to be persuaded enough to accept that there is no other sound on the planet aside from your speakers. However, this is just a large portion of the work done.

Complete accomplishment in MLM marketing comes when you can make your client to persuade other individuals likewise that there is no better stable on the world other than the ones that originate from your speakers. Along these lines you build up a lead just as get your products sold. This will help in building up both your deals and your enlisting market. This is one of the key significant factors in prevailing in a MLM business.

You ought to likewise be prepared to furnish your leads with any type of help if any is required. After deals administrations won't just pull in clients and leads yet in addition help to build your deals and get more benefits for you. Your MLM business framework ought to likewise be refreshed with the occasions to keep up the pace of achievement on the planet. It should utilize each cutting edge execute accessible to keep your business developing.

Online Versus Offline MLM Marketing Life Cycles

MLM has generally been alluded to as "verbal marketing" or "conversational marketing," which means you converse with individuals you know, loved ones, to advertise your MLM item or business. These individuals are your warm showcase.

Nowadays, however, many individuals are looking to the web as another channel for marketing MLM. With the intensity of social media locales like Twitter and Facebook, individuals are feeling the intensity of connecting and contacting individual's path outside their very own friend network.

Yet, as "social" as social media may show up, it's as yet a "chilly showcase," and numerous online MLM amateurs are finding the online marketing street rough and the going somewhat steep. The achievement rate appears to be low.

For what reason Don't My Online MLM Efforts Pay Off?

I get multiple messages seven days from individuals who ask me for what valid reason their online MLM endeavors don't appear to deliver any outcomes. These individuals are out there advancing their MLM business online with article marketing, pay-per-click, and any number of different techniques. So for what reason doesn't it appear to work?

The reality of the situation is that online MLM works. It just requires some investment. Like any virus marketing approach, online marketing has a more drawn out life cycle than marketing to your warm advertise. You likewise face a higher dismissal rate when you market to individuals who don't have any acquaintance with you, instead of individuals who do.

Online MLM Marketing Pros and Cons

Would it be a good idea for you to seek after online MLM marketing as advancement channel? We should investigate the advantages and disadvantages of online marketing.

Online Marketing Pros

- On the off chance that you make a blockhead of yourself your companions won't discover immediately, if at any point

- You can showcase online day in and day out, not exactly when individuals are conscious

- Even a withdrawn loner could utilize this strategy

- You generally don't confront dismissal face to face, you have absence of online traffic

- No compelling reason to dress "decent" for introductions

- It is minimal effort, since online marketing should be possible with for the most part real effort

- You can contact a lot a bigger number of individuals than one-on-one marketing with a warm showcase

- Online marketing can secure your protection in the event that regardless you work a normal everyday employment and don't need individuals to realize you are doing MLM

Online Marketing Cons

- The underlying absence of traffic to your website or blog can be exceptionally disheartening

- You regularly don't have the foggiest idea what you're fouling up in light of the fact that nobody lets you know (you manufactured it, they simply didn't come)

- It might require some investment to build up an online nearness, a significantly longer to build up a confided in online nearness

- It can any longer to get your underlying information exchanges

- You will presumably need to do some spearheading marketing without anyone else since most MLM organizations are not up to speed with powerful online marketing

Online MLM: Sleep, Creep, and Leap

So have I frightened you away yet? I would like to think not. Online MLM marketing is the flood of things to come for MLM marketing. The MLM business, up 'til now, simply hasn't made up for lost time with the substances of how to advertise online. As I have regularly stated, individuals who need to do online MLM need to gain from the best online advertisers outside the MLM business. Those individuals realize how to advertise anything online, MLM or not.

The online MLM life cycle is a ton like the existence cycle of your commonplace bamboo plant, which is rest, creep, and jump. The main year you plant bamboo, it just stays there and sits idle. It's resting. The horticulturists incorporate a little note with the bamboo revealing to you this is ordinary and not to freeze. The equivalent goes for online MLM. For the initial 50 blog entries you compose, your blog just rests. It stays there. Nothing occurs. Moan.

The second year in a bamboo vegetation's, it creeps. You'll see a couple of little shoots show up inches from the parent plant. The shoots are minor, yet in any event there is some obvious activity! Furthermore, you realize your bamboo plant didn't bite the dust. With a MLM blog, you'll see some jerk occurring, for the most part after your initial 50 posts. Individuals will begin to drop by and remark on your posts. Traffic to your blog and website get. Individuals start mentioning data and associating with you. Definitely! You're online endeavors are not dead in the water.

At long last, the third year of a bamboo vegetation's is one of excited activity: jump! Shoots begin showing up all over the place (even where you don't need them), and you begin pondering harm control so you don't wind up with bamboo in your yard. After around 100 blog entries, you've built up an online voice and your very own remarkable style. You get information exchanges for both the item and the business. You have built up a technique and procedure that works for you. Your business develops in jumps! You presently invest more energy showing others your strategy than marketing legitimately. Presently the influence of a MLM business truly begins to appear in your bonus check.

Bamboo and online MLM are comparable in their rest, creep, and jump cycles, however it doesn't frequently take 3 years to accomplish jump in MLM. Contingent upon how much time you can dedicate to marketing your MLM business online, hitting 100 blog entries may take path under 3 years.

Would you be able to wait for Online MLM Success?

Presently the inquiry progresses toward becoming whether you are persistent enough to hold up through rest and creep, to make it right to jump. Is it true that you are quiet enough to compose, post, and advance 100 online journals before your business detonates? It is safe to say that you will invest the energy to build up your own one of a kind online voice? Would you like to submit that much time and vitality?

A few people do and a few people don't. Whatever you pick, realizing the actualities in advance can truly help. What will you pick?

Sixteen Social Media Etiquette for MLM: The DOs

Beginning with social media behavior for business proprietors can be extreme. The steady advancement of social networks can make it hard to remain over prescribed procedures. Business proprietors who just every so often sign into these social networks may think that it's hard to completely see the majority of the subtleties that go about as unwritten use rules.

You'll see the most achievement when you have an equalization of human and business components. To help with accomplishing this equalization, a guide is made to utilizing Facebook, LinkedIn, and Twitter for business.

With regards to social media decorum for business, conduct and what to do or not do, it takes practice to completely see how these tips apply to your everyday conduct. Here are sixteen DOs with regards to social media decorum for business:

1. Complete and Update Your Social Media Profiles

Initial introductions are significant and enduring. Think about your social media accounts as your advanced initial introduction. Social media accounts that are just incompletely finished naturally show up less proficient. Take a couple of minutes to insightfully round out the entirety of your profile data – including contact data.

2. Separate Business and Personal Accounts

When building a business brand, it keeps your own and expert pages separate on social media. By being reliable with the kinds of substance you share by means of your business profile, your customers realize which record to pursue. You likewise abstain from spamming loved ones that tail you for individual updates.

For instance, a connection to your most recent blog entry should originate from your business page and a video of your canine in the terrace should originate from your own page.

3. Offer Thoughtfully

What you post turns into a portrayal of you and your business. Be glad for what your identity is and what you speak to as a business while remaining mindful of the picture you're creating because of the substance you share.

4. Post Regularly

This comes down to the unavoidable issue: how regularly would it be a good idea for you to draw in with your online network? This can fluctuate contingent upon your business and industry, yet it ought to be at any rate in any event a few times per week. This keeps crisp substance up front while opening up our customers' time. Customers can post without anyone else and are urged to do as such.

5. Organize Your Networks

It might entice to attempt each new social media stage that sprouts up, however it's hazardous to extend yourself excessively far. To begin, center around the social networks where you realize your clients are. More than likely, that is Facebook, LinkedIn, and either Instagram or Twitter. Giving quality substance through these outlets merits your time and exertion, regardless of your industry.

6. Associate with Your Audience

Giving supportive substance is pleasant, yet it's not every single social medium brings to the table. Connecting with your devotees is additionally key.

- See an inquiry or remark on Twitter that you can reply? Send the individual a cordial answer.

- Looking for proposals? Ask your Facebook group of spectators.

- Did you compose a supportive, industry-explicit post on your blog? Offer it with your LinkedIn network.

Manufacture associations online simply like you would face to face.

7. Be Transparent to Gain Trust

Should you keep running into an issue that causes a whirlwind of analysis on social media, the most noticeably terrible thing you can do is attempt and escape it. Attempt and react as well as can be expected, and don't wind up cautious. Work to cure the issue and let the individuals who thought about it online realize when it's settled

8. Help More Than You Sell

In spite of the fact that you're in business to profit, that shouldn't be the focal point of most by far of your social media posts. Keep the 80/20 standard as a primary concern here: 80 percent of the substance you post or offer ought to engage or useful, while close to 20 percent of your social media correspondence ought to legitimately identify with the merchandise or administrations you give.

9. Match the Right Content to the Right Network

Every social media network has its very own proposed reason and group of spectators. Getting this and coordinating your substance and tone to the correct social media outlet is basic for progress. Here's a breakdown: The easygoing network of Facebook makes commitment with others feel characteristic, while the business centered informing of LinkedIn offers the ideal spot to arrive at business experts. Twitter handles fast fire discussion between the two businesses and people, making it a helpful stage paying little mind to the target group.

10. Stay away from Poor Grammar and Spelling

Scarcely any things lessen your validity as fast as language structure missteps and spelling mistakes can. To help maintain a strategic distance from them, prep your social media refreshes in an archive or spreadsheet with spell check. You can likewise request that an associate edit before you share.

11. Be Visual

Photographs and recordings can help your social media methodology. Tweets that component pictures procure 150 percent more retweets are favorite 89 percent more and lead to 18 percent more snaps. On the off chance that your industry depends vigorously on visuals (like land or inside structure), consider including social media stages based visual commitment, as Instagram, to your marketing collection.

12. Area Tag Other Businesses

Social media is tied in with sharing. This implies most loved eateries, businesses, and different stops while you're all over the place. Make sure you add your area to your Instagram photograph or Facebook status so individuals know where you were and, all the more critically, how they can arrive. This is an inside and out great move to help different business proprietors and raise your image mindfulness inside the network.

13. Share without Expectations

Consistency and persistence will satisfy. When you begin placing time and exertion into social media doesn't mean you'll see enormous outcomes immediately. You may, and that is fantastic. Like beginning your business, your compass might be delayed from the start. At that point you'll make associations, manufacture a notoriety, and build up a methodology.

14. Give Credit When Credit Is Due

This is particularly valid on Twitter and Instagram. Remain on the correct side of social media decorum for business by ascribing the creator or picture taker when you share an intriguing tweet or a dazzling picture. Set aside the effort to discover the

Twitter handle in charge of the first post and incorporate it in your tweet.

Additionally, convey thank you tweets to the individuals who notice or retweet you. You can make some incredible associations when you play well with others on social media.

15. Think before Tagging

Labeling others in photographs is an extraordinary method to acquaint your business with their companions, yet before you do, thoroughly consider it. It is safe to say that you are labeling everybody you can consider on the grounds that you're trusting some of them will tail you or advance your business? Or on the other hand would you say you are labeling businesses and individuals to make a discourse or to feature something you appreciate about them? Sudden labeling can be a fun method to amaze and please somebody or could cost you companions, fans or adherents.

16. Have a ton of fun!

Utilizing social media for your business doesn't mean you should quit playing around with it! Have a ton of fun attempting new thoughts. Attempt live recordings or intuitive surveys and keep your messages proficient and conversational. You'll see that you can appreciate this piece of your business as opposed to fearing it.

DON'Ts on Social Media in MLM

Social media is an incredible method to advance your image, grow your compass, and increment devotees who will ideally progress toward becoming clients. In any case, it can likewise make inconvenience when not utilized effectively. One mix-up on Facebook, Twitter, Pinterest, or Google+, and your image is all of a sudden managing a genuine notoriety issue.

Since we don't need you to encounter that headache inciting bad dream, here are 30 things you ought to abstain from doing on social media:

1. Just Focusing on Facebook

When you consider social media, the main social network that rings a bell is most likely Facebook. With 71% of grown-ups online utilizing Facebook, it's anything but difficult to trust you can join Facebook and handle the majority of your social media needs from that point.

The issue is that Facebook may not be contacting your group of spectators. There are various social media stages more qualified for various crowds. LinkedIn is for experts, Vine is for the cool children.

While having a Facebook record ought to be a no-brainer, it shouldn't be your solitary social media network, either.

2. Hopping on Multiple Social Media Networks at Once

Despite the fact that you ought to be on different networks other than Facebook, having an excessive number of networks on the double can be similarly as adverse. Making accounts on Twitter, Pinterest, Google+, and Instagram and giving them a chance to stay lethargic won't help increment traffic to your website or devotees on social media. Also – how are you wanting to deal with each one of those records?

Rather, discover where your crowd invests a large portion of their energy. In the event that they have a huge nearness on Twitter, at that point you may not require a Pinterest account. Truth be told, your industry may not require picture based social media networks, so joining Pinterest or Instagram would be trivial.

3. Making it only about yourself

Consider that irritating companion or collaborator (we as a whole have one) who just discusses themselves. It gets old truly quick, and it makes you not have any desire to invest energy with that individual.

Something very similar applies to social media. In the event that everything you're doing is selling your item or administration, at that point that is a gigantic mood killer for individuals. Keep in mind, social media is most importantly social.

Albeit beginning on social media can be a test, remember it is tied in with beginning a discussion with individuals. Utilize social media to pose an inquiries or solicitation input from guests. It's these little activities that will cause individuals to tail you or your image.

4. Not Thinking Twice Before Posting

It's truly enticing to post an update when you have a battle with a friend or family member or representative. It's enticing to begin meandering about legislative issues after two or three beverages. However, when you update your status or convey that hostile tweet, it's there for eternity.

Being trained is troublesome on occasion, yet it's totally fundamental. The exact opposite thing you need to do is to irritate somebody. It's just going to ponder inadequately you and your image.

Continuously reconsider before sharing something on social media. What's more, on the off chance that you're furious or somewhat woozy, at that point ensure your telephone remains in your pocket.

5. Posting in a Hurry

Regardless of whether you simply had a splendid idea or need to be the primary individual to break some succulent bit of news, slowly inhale and think for a minute. Is the message suitable? Is it legitimate to share? Are the sources trusted? While this may not be as destroying in certain fields as in others, you simply need to post with an unmistakable head and not getting excessively energized.

For instance, you were in a washroom and heard individuals examine that a noteworthy merger would occur. First of all, they shouldn't share that out in the open, but on the other hand it's not your place to tweet that data. You're not Lois Lane.

We're not saying you ought to consider posts for quite a long time. Simply think before imparting delicious bits of data to the world.

6. Not Spell Checking

Counting contractions, abbreviations, and slang might be fine to use on an individual record with companions, yet not for an expert. Clients need to manage somebody who will really take the additional second to illuminate "you". It's a straightforward and compelling approach to demonstrate that you're an expert.

Moreover, twofold check your spellings. Between human mistake and auto-right, that one incorrectly spelled word can do real harm to your notoriety. Remember that individuals love to point these kind of mix-ups out, and that one minimal occurrence will live on in shame.

7. Reacting Unprofessionally

Since you are bantering with individuals—once more, social media is certainly not a single direction road—you will no doubt experience an individual who annoys you. Whatever you do, don't go all Amy's Bakery on them. That is totally amateurish and will just discolor your great name.

Continuously be considerate and aware. Regardless of whether you're not to blame, it's a mess simpler to murder them with consideration than to do harm control.

8. Being Impersonal

Show individuals there is really a person behind the record. A large portion of us really need to work with other individuals and not with ascertaining, aloof robots.

Give guests a superior comprehension of what your identity is by sharing your interests and qualities. In different woods, make individuals a "fan" of yours.

You can do this by being cheerful or clever. Think Taco Bell, Oreo, DiGiorno, or notwithstanding being progressively genuine and supporting something like a philanthropy run.

9. Avoiding Negative Comments/Controversy

Shockingly, you can't simply flee at whatever point you're looked with a test. Suppose you had a grammatical mistake or incidentally conveyed a tweet that was intended for individual use. It is imperative to possess ready. Individuals will really regard you for conceding you committed an error and have an educated an important exercise.

The Red Cross confronted a circumstance like this, yet really downplayed the situation, rather than disregarding it or posting one of those worn out expressions of remorse.

10. Not Listening

Some portion of making a network and really speaking with your adherents is setting aside the effort to peruse what individuals are stating about your image. There are a wide scope of free apparatuses that can accomplish this errand for you.

In the event that you see somebody has an inquiry or concern, set aside the effort to address the issue. You can likewise thank individuals who have positive things to state about your image.

11. Not Optimizing Social Media Profiles

On the off chance that you're acquainted with SEO, at that point this should bode well. Essentially, you ought to advance your social media profiles simply like you would your website. This implies you ought to have titles, depictions, and URLs that will perform well on both web search tools and social media.

Since every social media stage has various methods for upgrading profiles, you should audit this helpful article from Alex Chris. It traces the majority of the means that are required to enhance your Facebook, Twitter, Pinterest, and Google+ profiles.

12. Overlooking Social Media Buttons on Website

Make life simpler for you guests by including social media catches on your website. Along these lines, on the off chance that they like a bit of substance from your website, they can without much of a stretch offer it through their social media networks with only one straightforward snap.

These social media catches can likewise expand your image's perceivability and fans/devotees since once a guest pursues your Facebook, Twitter or LinkedIn accounts they'll get the most recent data you share.

HubSpot has an extraordinary "Extreme Cheat Sheet for Creating Social Media Buttons."

13. Being Too Casual

There might be times when you're clashed about the level of polished skill included. All things considered, generally, social media ought to be fun and intelligent.

Be that as it may, as we've referenced previously, you should keep up an expert relationship. In this way, referencing what you had for lunch most likely isn't generally going to help your image's social media nearness – except if you are a café.

We'll make reference to Taco Bell for instance once more. Taco Bell's social media nearness is fun and engaging. Be that as it may, somebody went excessively far and made a hostile comment. Taco Bell immediately quit fooling around and reported that it doesn't endure fanaticism.

14. Just Sharing Content from Your Website

Other than arriving at new clients and supporters, you're likewise utilizing social media to network inside your industry. This is the reason you ought to pursue industry pioneers and influencers and sharing their substance. This will in the long run help increment your adherents since you're somewhat riding on the coattails of built up and confided in people.

You need an assortment of substance that is useful or engaging for your group of spectators. Also, the most ideal approach to do that is by sharing adroit substance from power figures.

15. Being Inexperienced

Social media is at the intersection of ages. More youthful individuals have the experience and information to utilize social media, however they may come up short on the networking and relationship building abilities the more seasoned age has gained throughout the years. I'm not catching this' meaning?

It implies there are social media posts which would have never moved beyond experienced chiefs or administrators since they may not be proficient. This is the reason it's significant for everybody in your group to comprehend both the essentials of social media and the demonstrable skill important in the business world.

So, make certain everybody is in agreement when it's an ideal opportunity to share your image's dreams and qualities.

16. Expanding Amount of Followers Too Fast

While you unquestionably need to expand the measure of devotees you have on social media, you need to ensure you don't get such a large number of adherents too rapidly. Why? Since you're presumably accomplishing something against the principles if this occurs.

It's enticing to pursue the guidance of individuals who guarantee hundreds or thousands of new adherents in a short measure of time (frequently for 5, 10, or $20 bucks), however it is anything but a natural methodology. These stunts or hacks may convey new devotees for a minute, yet you could be face punishments—like not being permitted to include new companions or notwithstanding having your record suspended.

Additionally, a significant number of these "ensured genuine!" supporters are not individuals in your intended interest group. Seeing that number develop each time you sign in might feel better, it isn't really helping you contact individuals who will really bolster your image.

17. Leaving Comments Unattended

Let's face it here. There are some terrible individuals online who have nothing preferred to do over make your life as upsetting as could reasonably be expected. On the off chance that you don't address these individuals, otherwise known as trolls, they'll develop like weeds in a bloom bed. All things considered, it just takes that one remark for things to turn crazy.

Ensure that you address all remarks and grievances in an expert and opportune way. When managing a heckler, the best activity isn't to sink to their level and blow up. That is when things can get genuine terrible.

Salesforce.com has an accommodating aide for dealing with these circumstances.

18. Contracting a Social Media Manager Just Because They're "Well informed"

Because somebody is "educated", and knows it all on the specialized side of social media stages, doesn't mean they can deal with the obligations of a social media supervisor.

In some cases, procuring a marketing or correspondence master would be a superior alternative since they will have a superior comprehension of what your group of spectators is anticipating, your business targets, and the repercussions of a hostile post can be.

19. Depending on Just One Person

Making and sharing substance, alongside connecting with your crowd, on social media can occupy a ton of time and exertion. This is the reason you ought to have a social media group set up. Along these lines, on the off chance that somebody gets occupied with other work, your Facebook, Twitter, Google+, and other social media pages won't simply stay there inert.

Likewise, having a group set up methods you can react to clients and supporters on an all the more opportune premise. This is an incredible method to assemble your notoriety for being a brand devoted to client support.

20. Not Knowing the Difference between a Personal and Business Account

Did you realize that Facebook, Twitter, Pinterest and, Google+ have both individual and business pages? It's an incredible method to ensure you can have an individual and expert life on social media. Simply recollect, you will initially must have an individual profile and that regardless you should be cautious about what you post.

Notwithstanding, it allows somewhat more adaptability in demonstrating your character. In the event that you have representatives, ensure that they speak to your image by not sharing anything hostile.

21. Terrible Timing for Scheduled Posts

A large number of us have posts planned for development. It just makes life simpler to prepare.

Yet, imagine a scenario where there was an emergency. Suppose that you have a footwear organization and composed an article about the best Boston Marathon ever. You leave the post planned and afterward there was the awful assault during the Marathon. Your substance would appear to be uncouth on the grounds that individuals will trust you are attempting to take advantage of a disaster.

Continuously stay aware of the news, and if important, ensure you defer posts that are planned at unseemly occasions.

22. Not Creating Incentives

Continuously ensure that adherents are getting something out of your social media outlets. While challenges and complimentary gifts are demonstrated strategies, you don't generally need to give something endlessly. You could give convenient reactions, instructive guidance to better their lives, a sneak look at another item or even an in the background take a gander at your organization.

23. Thinking little of Data

What's the point in proceeding with your social media endeavors in the event that you don't have the foggiest idea how viable your battle is? What number of individuals did it reach? What substance intrigued your devotees the most? These are significant inquiries that should be replied through investigation.

24. Not Promoting Your Profiles through Advertising

This may come as a shock, yet not the majority of your supporters are going to get your posts. It was as of late uncovered that on the off chance that you had 1,000 likes on your Facebook page, at that point possibly 10 to 20 individuals will see your posts. This implies you may need to begin paying for promotions.

The majority of the real social media outlets offer promoting that can help increment your perceivability, which thus, can build more fans, preferences and supporters. Furthermore, it's really not so quite a bit of an expense.

25. Not Having a Check-and-Balance System in Place

Regardless of whether it's another arrangement of eyes to edit your status or ensuring a picture is suitable to share, it is anything but an impractical notion to have a check and parity framework set up. This implies preceding sharing substance on social media another person surveys it.

For instance, while you may believe that photos of everybody alcoholic during the workplace Christmas Party is an extraordinary method to adapt your image, another person may advise you that those pictures aren't average and can send an inappropriate impression of your organization.

This shouldn't shield content from being inventive or shared rapidly, it just ought to be a safeguard to keep your image from living in a PR bad dream.

26. Being a Debbie Downer or Negative Nancy

Experience the Newsfeed of your Facebook account. Which statuses would you say you are bound to peruse? The ones respecting the introduction of a youngster, getting a charge out of multi day at the shoreline, or sharing a persuasive picture? Or then again the statuses griping about work, being wiped out or exactly how horrible life is?

For the most part, we're progressively disposed to peruse and react to inspiration on social media. Rather than slamming the challenge or spreading antagonism, share content that is elevating, helpful, or cheerful. This sort of substance is bound to be seen and shared.

To put it plainly, positive substance is more important than negative substance.

27. Being Inconsistent

There's a rhyme and motivation to when and how much content you share on social media. For instance, you ought to find the best occasions when your group of spectators is online.

In the event that that happens to be Monday through Thursday at 5:00, at that point that is the point at which you ought to post content—and that should be all the time.

Individuals will start to expect seeing your updates at specific occasions ordinary. In the event that you get out from under that propensity for even only seven days, your devotees are probably going to disregard you and proceed onward.

28. Neglecting to Create 'Validness'

Another method for putting this is "don't discuss it, be about it."

Clients need to accept you're a specialist in your industry. They need to accept the products or administrations you give are those you would use also.

In the event that you broadcast yourself as a naturally mindful brand, at that point don't dump garbage or concoction squander in a lake. Be straightforward and consistently try to do you say others should do.

29. Posting without Images/Videos

You've presumably seen a ton of substance comprises of either pictures or recordings. That is on the grounds that these visual bits of substance are quicker for us to process (multiple times quicker than content) and are effectively sharable.

Having an amazing picture or video can likewise expand the measure of preferences for your post. On Facebook, for instance, pictures are loved twice to such an extent.

30. Ill-advised Use of Hashtags

Hashtags have turned out to be such a wonder, that they're regularly taunted (that Jimmy Fallon and Justin Timberlake sketch is as yet incredible however). Be that as it may, hashtags can give your social media content a noteworthy lift.

It was discovered that when brands utilize a hashtag on Twitter, commitment can increment by 50 percent. This is an incredible method to extend your range. Hashtags likewise serve a similarly significant job on Facebook, Pinterest, and Google+.

You would prefer not to try too hard with hashtags. Having an excessive number of hashtags looks jumbled and frantic, so utilize significant hashtags with some restraint. Additionally, ensure that it's clear.

Utilizing something like #thisiswaytoolongasentencetouseashashtag is simply silly! Nobody can peruse that. Keep it basic and to the point.

CHAPTER FIVE

USING SOCIAL MEDIA TO FIND PROSPECTS

Social media marketing is the utilization of social media stages to interface with your crowd to fabricate your image, increment deals, and drive website traffic. This includes distributing incredible substance on your social media profiles, tuning in to and connecting with your supporters, dissecting your outcomes, and running social media ads.

The significant social media stages (right now) are Facebook, Instagram, Twitter, LinkedIn, Pinterest, YouTube, and Snapchat.

There are additionally a scope of social media the board devices that help businesses to capitalize on the social media stages recorded previously. For instance, Buffer is a foundation of social media the executive instruments, which can enable you to make progress with your social media marketing.

Social media marketing initially began with distributing. Businesses were sharing their substance on social media to produce traffic to their websites and, ideally, deals. In any case, social media has developed a long ways past being only a spot to communicate content.

These days, businesses utilize social media in a bunch of various ways. For instance, a business that is worried about what individuals are stating about its image would screen social media discussions and reaction to significant notices (social media tuning in and commitment). A business that needs to see how it's performing on social media would break down its scope, commitment, and deals on social media with an investigation instrument (social media examination). A business that needs to arrive at a particular arrangement of group of spectators at scale would run exceptionally focused on social media advertisements (social media publicizing).

All in all, these are regularly otherwise called social media the executives.

1. Technique

Before you make a plunge and distribute something on social media, we should make a stride back and take a gander at the master plan. The initial step is to consider your social media procedure.

What are your objectives? In what manner can social media help you accomplish your business objectives? A few businesses utilize social media for expanding their image mindfulness, others use it for driving website traffic and deals. Social media can likewise enable you to produce commitment around your image, make a network, and fill in as a client bolster channel for your clients.

Which social media stages would you like to concentrate on? The real social media stages, referenced are Facebook, Instagram, Twitter, LinkedIn, Pinterest, YouTube, and Snapchat. There are additionally littler and exceptional stages, for example, Tumblr, Tik Tok, and Anchor, and social informing stages, for example, Messenger, WhatsApp, and WeChat. When beginning, it's smarter to pick a couple of stages that you think your intended interest group is on than to be on all stages.

What sort of substance would you like to share? What sort of substance will draw in your intended interest group best? Is it pictures, recordings, or connections? Is it instructive or engaging substance? A decent spot to begin is to make a marketing persona, which will enable you to address these inquiries. Furthermore, this doesn't need to be fixed perpetually; you can generally change your procedure as per how your social media posts perform.

To enable you to make an extraordinary social media procedure, here are our long-structure, well ordered aides on making a social media methodology and social media marketing plan.

2. Arranging and Publishing

Social media marketing for private ventures for the most part begins with having a predictable nearness on social media. Near three billion individuals (3,000,000,000!) utilize social media. By being available on social media stages, you offer your image a chance to be found by your future clients.

Distributing to social media is as basic as sharing a blog entry, a picture, or a video on a social media stage. It's much the same as how you would share on your own Facebook profile. Be that as it may, you will need to prepare of time as opposed to making and distributing content immediately. Likewise, to guarantee that you are amplifying your range on social media, you have to distribute incredible substance that your crowd likes, at the correct planning and recurrence.

There are presently an assortment of social media planning instruments, for example, Buffer Publish, that can enable you to distribute your substance naturally at your favored time. This spares you time and enables you to contact your group of spectators when they are destined to connect with your substance.

3. Tuning in and Engagement

As your business and social media following develop, discussions about your image will likewise increment. Individuals will remark on your social media posts, label you in their social media posts, or message you legitimately.

Individuals may even discuss your image on social media without telling you. So you will need to screen social media discussions about your image. In the event that it's a positive remark, you get an opportunity to astound and please them. Else, you can offer help and right a circumstance before it deteriorates.

You can physically check every one of your warnings over all the social media stages yet this isn't effective and you won't see posts that didn't label your business' social media profile. You can rather utilize a social media tuning in and commitment.

4. Examination

Regardless of whether you are distributing content or connecting on social media, you will need to know how your social media marketing is performing. It is safe to say that you are contacting a bigger number of individuals on social media than a month ago? What number of positive notices do you get a month? What number of individuals utilized your image's hashtag on their social media posts?

The social media stages themselves give an essential level of such data. To get more top to bottom examination data or to effortlessly look at crosswise over social media stages, you can utilize the wide scope of social media investigation devices accessible, for example, Buffer Analyze (in shut beta).

5. Promoting

When you have more assets to develop your social media marketing, a territory that you can consider is social media promoting. Social media advertisements enable you to contact a more extensive group of spectators than the individuals who are tailing you.

Social media publicizing stages are so amazing these days that you can determine precisely who to show your advertisements to. You can make target spectators dependent on their socioeconomics, interests, practices, and that's just the beginning.

When you are running numerous social media publicizing efforts on the double, you can consider utilizing a social media promoting instrument to make mass changes, computerize forms, and streamline your advertisements.

MLM Success Tips: What you Need When Joining a Network Marketing Business

Utilize these MLM achievement tips to guarantee you land at the top. Network marketing is probably the quickest approaches to manufacture genuine, long haul riches. Notwithstanding, on the off chance that you don't know about the key variables of making a flourishing association, your MLM achievement could be immediately imperiled. Most network advertisers quit inside 90 days. So as to ascend to the highest point of your MLM organization, and be in the top 3% in the business, you should have these 5 key MLM achievement tips as they are basic for your MLM achievement.

#1: An Expert: When an individual joins a MLM business, they need a specialist that can enable them to succeed. Sure they are amped up for the item or may have positive item results, however what they truly need is a specialist. Discovering this master enables them to likewise feel good in supporting new reps. They comprehend they don't need to be the master yet, in light of the fact that they can depend upon you or even your upline, while they are learning and enrolling.

#2: A System: New MLM reps need a framework set up to assistance them assemble their business. They need a business channel that leads and prospects can experience. One that assembles and makes trust and trust in the MLM agent. I am not discussing the equivalent reproduced website that each other merchant has. Those are essentially customer facing facades and they are not one of a kind and they don't offer some incentive. That ought to really be the last place a lead turned prospect should wind up - and that is the point at which they are at long last prepared to buy or go along with you. A 'framework' is basic to your business and your MLM achievement.

#3: More Leads Equals More Money: Generating leads is basic to your MLM achievement. MLM reps should discover prospects to converse with. You would prefer not to pursue, dog and weight your warm advertise. It is savvy to utilize a referral play prospecting procedure on your warm market and after that proceed onward to those that are searching for you. At some point or another, all MLM reps come up short on their warm advertise. New reps need an interminable stream of prompts converse with. What's more, far and away superior, those leads need an enthusiasm for something you bring to the table; a specialist, a framework, administration, your MLM business, and so forth.

#4: Recruiting New Reps Weekly: Let's face it, the money is in enrolling and duplication. You need your reps to do what you are doing. In the event that it's not penniless, don't fix it. On the off chance that you need a flourishing MLM business, you have to enlist 2-5 reps week by week. What's more, your reps should do likewise. Doing this will make them overwhelm your MLM. It is conceivable in the event that you have a framework as referenced previously. It is safe to say that you are in it to win it and prepared to walk the phase at your next MLM occasion, or would you rather be sitting in the group of spectators constantly? I suspected as much. You need to command! Furthermore, you will, in the event that you pursue these basic MLM achievement tips.

#5: Leadership: It's the most smoking quality on earth today! New MLM reps search for pioneers to help control them in their MLM achievement. A pioneer will help lead you down the correct way. A pioneer will enable you to realize what you have to know to be fruitful in your MLM business. To profit in your MLM business, you have to turn into the Expert and the Leader. Do you know how?

Remember, your item and friends might be excellent, however, the way to progress exists in you and what you can give to those that you acquire to your business.

On the off chance that you ace these MLM Success Tips, at that point you will most likely move to the top and rule your MLM.

The most effective method to create a Social Media Marketing Strategy Easy Steps for MLM

A social media marketing system is an outline of all that you intend to do and would like to accomplish on social media. It controls your activities and tells you whether you're succeeding or falling flat. Each post, answer, as, and remark should fill a need.

The more explicit your methodology is, the more successful the execution will be. Keep it compact. Try not to make your arrangement so grandiose and wide that it's unattainable or difficult to gauge.

Stage 1. Set social media marketing objectives that adjust to business destinations

Set S.M.A.R.T. objectives

The initial step to making a triumphant procedure is to set up your targets and objectives. Without objectives, you have no real way to quantify achievement or rate of profitability (ROI).

Every one of your objectives ought to be:

- Specific
- Measurable
- Attainable
- Relevant
- Time-bound

This is the S.M.A.R.T. objective structure. It will direct your activities and guarantee they lead to genuine business results.

Track significant measurements

Vanity measurements like retweets and preferences are anything but difficult to follow, yet it's difficult to demonstrate their genuine worth. Rather, center rather around targets, for example, leads created, web referrals, and transformation rate.

For motivation, investigate these 19 fundamental social media measurements.

You might need to follow various objectives for various channels, or even various employments of each channel. For instance, Benefit Cosmetics drives brand mindfulness with its paid social crusades, yet measures securing and commitment for natural social posts.

Make a point to adjust your social media objectives to your general marketing technique. This will make it simpler for you to demonstrate the estimation of your work and get official purchase in and speculation.

Stage 2. Get the hang of all that you can about your group of spectators

Make group of spectators personas

Knowing who your group of spectators—and perfect client—is and what they need to see on social is critical to making content that they will like, remark on, and share. It's additionally basic on the off chance that you need to transform social media supporters into clients for your business.

Have a go at making group of spectators/purchaser personas. These enable you to think about your potential fans, adherents, and clients as genuine individuals with genuine needs and needs. What's more, that will enable you to think all the more unmistakably about what to offer them.

Accumulate certifiable information

Social media investigation can likewise give a huge amount of profitable data about who your supporters are, the place they live, which dialects they talk, and how they interface with your image on social. These bits of knowledge enable you to refine your methodology and better focus on your social advertisements.

Stage 3. Research the challenge

Chances are, your rivals are as of now utilizing social media—and that implies you can gain based on what's going on with as of now.

Lead an aggressive investigation

An aggressive examination enables you to comprehend who the challenge is and what they're progressing nicely (and not all that well). You'll get a decent feeling of what's normal in your industry, which will enable you to set social media focuses of your own.

This examination will likewise enable you to spot openings. For instance, perhaps one of your rivals is overwhelming on Facebook, however has placed little exertion into Twitter or Instagram. You should concentrate on the networks where your group of spectators is underserved, as opposed to attempting to win fans from an overwhelming player.

Take part in social tuning in

Social listening is another approach to watch out for the challenge. Here's the manner by which to utilize Hootsuite streams for social tuning in and observing contenders:

As you track contender accounts and applicable industry catchphrases, you may notice moves in the manner these stations are utilized. Or on the other hand, you may recognize a particular post or crusade that truly hits the imprint—or thoroughly bombs. Watch out for this data and use to it assess your own objectives and plans.

Stage 4. Direct a social media review

Inspect your present endeavors

In case you're as of now utilizing social media instruments, you have to make a stride back and see what you've officially done and achieved. Ask yourself the accompanying inquiries:

- What's working, and so forth?
- Who is interfacing with you on social?
- Which networks does your intended interest group use?
- How does your social media nearness contrast with that of your rivals?

When you accumulate this data in a single spot, you'll have a decent beginning stage for arranging how to improve your outcomes.

Your review should give you a reasonable picture of what reason every one of your social records serves. On the off chance that the motivation behind a record isn't clear, consider whether it merits keeping.

To enable you to choose, ask yourself the accompanying inquiries:

1. Is my group of spectators here?
2. If all in all, how are they utilizing this stage?
3. Can I utilize this record to help accomplish important business objectives?

Posing these extreme inquiries will help keep your system on track and centered.

Search for impostor accounts

During the review you may find false records utilizing your business name or the names of your products.

These frauds can be hurtful to your image, don't worry about it catching devotees that ought to be yours. Report them. You might need to get your Facebook and Twitter records confirmed to guarantee your fans and devotees realize they are managing the genuine you.

Stage 5. Set up records and improve existing profiles

Figure out which networks to utilize (and how to utilize them)

As you choose which social channels to utilize, you will likewise need to characterize your procedure for each network.

It's a decent exercise to make statements of purpose for each network. These one-sentence revelations will enable you to concentrate on an unmistakable objective for each record on every social network.

Model: "We will utilize Facebook publicizing to focus on a particular group of spectators so as to build deals." One more: "We will utilize Instagram for advancing and sharing our organization culture to help with enrollment and representative promotion."

In the event that you can't make a strong statement of purpose for a specific social network, you might need to reevaluate whether that network is justified, despite all the trouble.

Set up (and streamline) your records

When you've chosen which networks to concentrate on, it's an ideal opportunity to make your profiles—or improve existing profiles so they line up with your key arrangement.

- Make sure you round out all profile fields
- Use watchwords individuals will use to scan for your business
- Use pictures that are accurately measured for each network

Try not to give this rundown a chance to overpower you. Keep in mind, it's smarter to utilize less channels well than to extend yourself slender attempting to keep up a nearness on each network.

Stage 6. Discover motivation

While it's significant that your image be exceptional, you can in any case draw motivation from different businesses that are incredible on social.

Social network examples of overcoming adversity

You can for the most part discover these on the business segment of the social network's website. (Here's Facebook's, for instance.)

These contextual investigations can offer important experiences you can apply to your very own objectives for every social network.

Grant winning records and crusades

You could likewise look at the champs of The Facebook Awards or The Shorty Awards for instances of brands that are at the highest point of their social media game.

Your preferred brands on social media.

Who do you appreciate following on social media? What do they do that constrains individuals to draw in and share their substance?

National Geographic, for instance, is truly outstanding on Instagram, consolidating shocking visuals with convincing subtitles.

Notice that every one of these records has a reliable voice, tone, and style. Consistency is vital to helping your supporters comprehend what's in store from your image. They'll know why they should keep on tailing you and what worth they will get from doing as such. It likewise helps keep your marking predictable notwithstanding when you have multiple individuals taking a shot at your social group.

For additional on this, read our guide on building up a convincing brand 'voice' on social media.

Ask your supporters

Customers can likewise offer social media motivation. What are your objective clients discussing online? What would you be able to find out about their needs and needs? In the event that you have existing social channels, you could likewise ask your current adherents what they need from you. Simply ensure that you finish and convey what they request.

Stage 7. Make a social media substance schedule

Sharing extraordinary substance is basic, obviously, however it's similarly imperative to have an arrangement set up for when you'll share substance to get the greatest effect. Your social media substance schedule additionally needs to represent the time you'll go through connecting with the crowd (in spite of the fact that you have to take into account some unconstrained commitment also).

Make a posting plan

Your social media substance schedule records the dates and times at which you will distribute kinds of substance on each channel. It's the ideal spot to design the majority of your social media exercises—from pictures and connection sharing to blog entries and recordings. It incorporates both your everyday posting and substance for social media crusades. Your schedule guarantees your posts are scattered suitably and distributed at the ideal occasions.

Plot your substance blend

Ensure your schedule mirrors the statement of purpose you've doled out to every social profile, so that all that you post is attempting to help your business objectives. For instance, you may choose that:

- 50 percent of substance will drive traffic back to your blog
- 25 percent of substance will be curated from different sources
- 20 percent of substance will bolster venture objectives (selling, lead age, and so forth.)
- 5 percent of substance will be about HR and friends culture

Putting these diverse post types in your substance schedule will help guarantee you keep up the proportion you've arranged. In case you're beginning without any preparation and you're just not certain what sorts of substance to post, attempt the 80-20 guideline:

- 80 percent of your posts ought to illuminate, teach, or engage your group of spectators
- 20 percent can legitimately advance your image.

You could likewise attempt the social media standard of thirds:

- One-third of your social substance advances your business, changes over perusers, and produces benefit.

- One-third of your social substance shares thoughts and stories from idea pioneers in your industry or similar businesses.

- One-third of your social substance includes individual connections with your group of spectators.

When you have your schedule set, use planning instruments or mass booking to set up your informing ahead of time instead of refreshing always for the duration of the day. This enables you to make the language and organization of your posts as opposed to keeping in touch with them on the fly at whatever point you have time.

Stage 8. Test, assess, and modify your technique

Your social media procedure is a gigantically significant record for your business, and you can't expect you'll get it precisely directly on the primary attempt. As you actualize your arrangement and track your outcomes, you may locate that a few methodologies don't function just as you'd foreseen, while others are working far and away superior to anticipate.

Track your information

Notwithstanding the investigation inside every social network (see Step 2), you can utilize UTM parameters to follow social guests as they travel through your website, so you can see precisely which social posts drive the most traffic to your website.

Rethink, test, and do everything once more

When this information begins coming in, use it to reconsider your procedure routinely. You can likewise utilize this data to test various posts, crusades, and procedures against each other. Steady testing enables you to comprehend what works and what doesn't, so you can refine your methodology continuously.

Studies can likewise be an extraordinary method to discover how well your system is functioning. Ask your supporters, email rundown, and website guests whether you're living up to their needs and desires, and what they'd like to see a greater amount of. At that point make a point to convey on what they let you know.

In the social circle, things change quickly. New networks develop, while others experience critical statistic shifts. Your business will experience times of progress also. The majority of this implies your social media methodology ought to be a living report that you take a gander at routinely and alter as required. Allude to it regularly to keep you on track, yet don't be reluctant to improve changes with the goal that it reflects new objectives, devices, or plans.

When you update your social technique, try to tell everybody in your group. That way they would all be able to cooperate to enable your business to benefit as much as possible from your social media accounts.

CHAPTER SIX

HOW TO REACH OUT TO SOMEONE ON SOCIAL MEDIA

Today with the economy the most noticeably terrible it's been in years numerous individuals are racing to MLM. In spite of the fact that the economy is in a decay the MLM business is blasting every one of those individuals who used to think MLM was some sort of trick or fraudulent business model are currently observing the excellence of MLM.

MLM (Multi-Level Marketing) is a long way from dead and will be around for a considerable length of time to come. The idea of MLM enables somebody to take their budgetary future in their very own hands and make the measure of salary they need. You're working for the best individual to work for "YOURSELF".

Despite the fact that MLM there's no constrained to the measure of money you can make it takes want, hard work and understanding key ideas to succeed.

In MLM you get paid for one thing enrolling. On the off chance that you don't see how to manufacture a business, you will never get the prizes in MLM.

Truly my long stretches of experience doing MLM has shown me the most ideal approach to manufacture your MLM business is online. Here are a few advantages of structure your business online.

- Less time to get more outcomes
- You can fabricate your business all inclusive
- You can maintain your business all day, every day even while you rest.
- You can without much of a stretch objective individuals who need what you have

The Breakdown of What You Need To Know To Dominate In MLM

The truth is 90 percent of the individuals who are in MLM are coming up short. This is basically in light of the fact that they never figure out how to showcase. A great many people simply join a MLM organization and imagine that is it. On the off chance that it was that simple everybody would be tycoons in MLM.

So what does it take to assemble a prosperous business? Here are some MLM Recruiting Tips that will open your eyes...

Center - Whatever business marketing techniques you pick you should be focused. Many individuals jump from chance to circumstance, marketing procedure to marketing system, on the off chance that you treating your MLM like you have ants in your jeans your business will never be steady. You have to concentrate on one chance and a couple of marketing procedures until you're getting a few outcomes.

Each marketing procedure works individuals simply don't stay with them long enough to get results.

Consistency - You as a business proprietor must be predictable. In case you're getting down to business your business low maintenance or full time, there must be reliable time during the time you're taking a shot at your business. Much the same as you have a calendar for your activity you should make one for your business. Keep in mind on the off chance that you treat your business like a business it will remunerate you like one.

Lead Capture Page - This is so significant; I truly don't perceive how you can work a useful business online without one. Leads are really the backbone of any business. You need a lead catch page to catch traffic.

Automated assistant - This is the manner by which you're going to put your business on autopilot. An automated assistant does the truly difficult work for your business. You can actually fabricate relationships, train individuals, and showcase your business to a huge number of individuals with never conversing with them.

An automated assistant is additionally a database where you construct your very own rundown of leads. With an automated assistant you control the data, which is incredible and will do ponders for your business.

Directed Traffic - Once you have your lead catch or Blog, you need to focused on traffic. The just way you will get focused on traffic is through predictable marketing. Social networks, Video sharing locales, SEO, Forums, ad Words, Articles these marketing techniques can bring you laser focused on traffic for your business.

Keep in mind you don't have to realize each marketing procedure out there you just need to turn into a marketing expert with a couple of them.

Marking - Branding is another key segment to progress. Most MLM or network marketing organizations give you a repeated website. Imagine if all of us seemed to be similar what sort of world would it be?

The equivalent looks good for your business the main way you going to stand apart is by marking yourself. You're remarkable in your own specific manner of share in marketing and watch how this changes your business.

When you have these segments chipping away at a regular routine for your business enrolling individuals into your MLM will come simple. This is the equation for selecting a boundless measure of individuals in your MLM...

Steps to a "Master Style" Online MLM Business

On the off chance that you need to assemble a viable online MLM business it's of basic significance that you situating yourself as a specialist and that you likewise put your message before however many laser focused on prospects as could reasonably be expected regularly. Here are a few stages that you can pursue, and simultaneously duplicate the best Internet MLM whizzes out there today:

1.) Target Other Network Marketers And Make Easy Money By Recommending Products That They Are Buying Anyway: As a network advertiser your best market is other network advertisers, so you should position yourself to profit from the whole network marketing industry, where you for instance sell your very own nonexclusive MLM products and courses to them. Take a gander at the best online MLM whizzes out there today, and you'll understand. For them it doesn't generally make a difference if individuals join their essential MLM program or not, on the grounds that they profit from the whole network marketing industry at any rate.

The "MLM Gurus" make pain free income by selling products that actually all network advertisers needs and purchases at any rate. Products like for instance: Their Own Generic MLM Products, Courses, Leads and Traffic programs, Site expenses, Auto-responder memberships, Hosting, and so on. Along these lines, while the "MLM Guru" makes simple money, the other 95% of all network advertisers going around on the "combat zone" and attempting to pitch each other on various MLM openings.

The "MLM Guru" has basically figured out how to help other network advertisers by tackling their most concerning issues. Rather than marketing and selling his essential MLM program, he has figured out how to "unravel" and "serve", where he offers his own products and courses to other network advertisers. By doing this he position himself as a specialist and win people groups trust and regard, and they will be increasingly open to work with him.

The "MLM Guru" comprehends that Network advertisers are as of now burning through money on data that can assist them with getting their MLM business to push ahead. Along these lines, here they can make simple money by offering courses to them on for instance: "How To Build An Effective Online MLM Business".

2.) Set Up a http://www.YourName.com Website: Your genuine business is YOU! Your message, your story, your character, your voice, and so on. So something else that is significant once you are building your online MLM business is that you set up an expert website in YourName.com. This will assist you with branding yourself and to stand apart from every one of the majority out there. Once more, in the event that you take a gander at the best "Web MLM Superstars" out there today, at that point you can see that they all have comprehended the significance with having their very own website, where they essentially showcase and advance themself.

3.) Set Up A Generic MLM Website Where You Position Yourself As A Leader, And Where You Offer Free Generic MLM Training To The Entire Network Marketing Industry:

A compelling online MLM business must have a situation with incredible Free assets, for example, Membership destinations, Toll Free Numbers, Audio and Video preparing, Conferance calls, Webinars, and so on. Here you can offer Generic MLM preparing to the whole network marketing industry. By doing that you will mark yourself and win people groups trust and regard, and lead them in to your "Business pipe", where you can demonstrate to them your different products.

If you don't offer Generic MLM preparing, at that point you can't focus on the large number of network advertisers out there that have "NO" enthusiasm to join your specific MLM program. Keep in mind that, over 95% surprisingly bomb in network marketing, and the huge greater part of those individuals are searching for a Leader. Thus, when they have acknowledged you to be their Leader, at that point a considerable lot of those individuals will go along with you.

4.) Set up a Blog and Position Yourself as The Person in Your Primary MLM Program to go to for Help and Advice: When individuals are looking on the Internet for data about your essential MLM program, at that point you clearly need them to discover you. Extraordinary compared to other approach to achieve that will be that you set up a Blog where you post news and updates about your essential MLM organization. The Google Algorithm adores Blogs, so your Blog will get recorded rapidly and chances are that you are only one of only a handful couple of individuals in your MLM organization that uses this system. Likewise recall that, individuals that are looking for data on the Internet right now about your essential MLM program is your most focused on market, since they are as of now pre sold on your essential MLM organization and opportunity.

The network marketing industry will consistently be near, and other network advertisers will consistently be searching for more Leads and additionally Training. The basic truth is that other network advertisers will consistently be enthusiastic on the best way to become familiar with the mysteries on for instance: How to support more individuals and how to get more Leads to contact for their essential network marketing opportunity.

As of now, there are more than one billion individuals on the Internet and in all actuality your best prospects can be discovered online, on the grounds that there is the place they do their looking in any case. In this way, truly all network advertisers out there today are keen on a guide that can show them how to fabricate a viable online MLM business.

MLM Lead Generation-How to Generate Free MLM Leads For Your MLM Business

There's totally one thing you should have so as to become your MLM business and that is leads. You need huge amounts of focused MLM leads. The main issue is, how would you create leads for your MLM business? Indeed, I'm going to share some MLM lead age methods that will tell you the best way to produce free focused on MLM leads for your business.

With regards to producing leads for your MLM business, it can get extravagant. The MLM lead age tips I'm going to impart to you will enable you to produce MLM leads for nothing. That way, regardless of whether you're on a financial limit, you will at present have the option to develop your business. Really cool stuff, correct?

MLM Lead Generation Tip #1

Utilizing the web, beyond a shadow of a doubt, is a ground-breaking approach to become your MLM business. It'll take your business and transform it into a MLM lead creating machine. One approach to do this is to utilize video marketing (model: YouTube.com, it's free and simple to utilize). Utilizing this method will enable you to create several focused on MLM leads for your business.

When setting up your video, you should give away free supportive data. Model would be if market travel, you can give tips on arranging an extraordinary excursion. What's more, toward the part of the bargain, you can give your website, telephone number or email address. This will have individuals calling you who are not kidding about going along with you in your MLM business.

MLM Lead Generation Tip #2

Another cool and free approach to transform your MLM business into a MLM lead age machine is by utilizing online journals. You can get a free blog at blogger.com. Sites will enable you to produce many focused on MLM leads every day for your business.

When setting up your blog, you should discuss the advantages of utilizing the products or administration. Likewise, give out a couple of additional tips and data that individuals could use to accomplish whatever outcome they're searching for. On the off chance that you decide to, you can add pictures to your blog. What's more, remember to include your telephone number or email address. You'll unquestionably have individuals calling you or messaging you needing more data about your business. This will bring about you creating a huge amount of profoundly focused on MLM leads.

MLM Lead Generation Tip #3

Another approach to create MLM leads for your business is by composing official statements. You can submit them at free at PrLog.com. When composing your public statement, you should discuss some newsworthy. Or on the other hand on the off chance that you have another item turning out. Or on the other hand in case you're 'running contrary to the natural order of things'. Composing official statements will produce MLM leads for you. What's more, help make developing your business fun and energizing.

Utilize these MLM lead age tips to create free MLM leads for your business. When you do, you'll include many individuals into your MLM business on a week by week premise, regardless of whether you're on a spending limit.

MLM Training - How to Convince People That Your Business Is Professional

In many cases, prospects can rush to the draw and shout, "Is this one of those pyramids?" or "Network Marketing doesn't work!" before you even get an opportunity to inform them concerning your incredible products or business. Here's some strong MLM preparing and contents you can use to legitimately and expertly get your prospects past the MLM protest.

In this article you will figure out how to persuade your prospects that your MLM business is genuine and proficient, and not only a pyramid or a trick. And afterward we'll finish up with some MLM preparing contents you can use to direct your discussions when a prospect has a protest about network marketing.

MLM or network marketing questions or complaints will come to you by your prospect asking, "Is this MLM?" "Is this Network Marketing?" Or, "Is this one of those pyramids?" Or, "Is this like Amway, Mary Kay or some other organization?"

This inquiry/protest comes up from the prospect being recently presented to MLM/Network marketing or by catching wind of it through somebody, for example, a companion, relative or from the media. To appropriately deal with this complaint - on the off chance that it is a protest - you will do what you generally do on an inquiry or protest and that is to discover what their experience has been. Ordinarily they've had none, all their data is prattle.

In the event that they have had an awful involvement with MLM, the best way to get past this protest is to direct them to see that their awful experience or absence of achievement was a result of inadequate MLM preparing. Regardless of whether the organization they were engaged with left business, the reason is as yet absence of successful MLM preparing - all things considered it would have been poor preparing on the most proficient method to assess an organization.

Along these lines, to outline how to deal with the MLM protest you initially should discover what their experience has been, and after that guide them to understanding that their absence of achievement or terrible experience was because of poor preparing.

Presently on the off chance that they've never been associated with network marketing and all their data is gossip, pursue similar strategies. You take each issue they raise and demonstrate to them how appropriate MLM preparing settles it. Clearly in the event that they raise that it's unlawful, you would deal with that by having them watch Brilliant Compensation. I've never gotten a pyramid complaint after the prospect has viewed the Brilliant Compensation video.

WORDS TO USE

To help manage you through this technique - allude to the downloaded stream outline while you read this:

Prospect asks, "Is this MLM?"

"Indeed it is MLM - how are you aware of?"

Or then again,

"Can you explain what you mean by MLM?"

At that point the following significant inquiry is, "Do you have individual involvement with a MLM organization or would you say you are alluding to another person's understanding?"

Ordinarily you don't need to ask this since they would have addressed it inside their reaction to your first question. Be that as it may, ensure you know. I can't reveal to you how often I went jumping into taking care of this complaint before I discovered that they had never at any point been engaged with it. In the event that they have not been included, yet have a negative perspective on the business you should display FACTS about the business.

When they have had involvement with network marketing, you need to let them completely reveal to you their experience - recognize all that they state - never contend or can't help contradicting them. Never talk severely about another organization or upline. When you have all the data, at that point continue with this inquiry:

"Networks marketing work...not for you, not for anybody you know...just does it as an industry work?" (Get their reaction.)

At that point ask, "What do you think it takes for it to work for an individual?" And from here you should control them to preparing. Truly attempt to have them see and express that preparation is the main clear arrangement. Do whatever it takes not to TELL them this, control them to it and get them to acknowledge and state it on their own. Keep in mind, on the off chance that you state it - it very well may be tested; on the off chance that they state it - it must be valid.

Okay, when they concur that powerful MLM preparing is the arrangement, disclose to them the preferred position they will have with your special preparing (I do suggest you talk about what you've discovered with Professional Inviter in light of the fact that this is altogether different preparing than most have ever gotten in network marketing and it is really what they need). Presently, you must get them to see how this time is different than the last time or times they were involved with MLM.

In the event that they don't perceive how it's unique, they won't go along with you. After you've gotten them to concur that preparation is the arrangement and yours is extraordinary - at that point you near activity with something like:

"Imprint, I need to plunk down with you and demonstrate to you how it's extraordinary. I need to demonstrate to you the preparation devices that are presently accessible to you. Is it true that you are available to plunking down?"

An option would be:

"Imprint, all that you've raised here I thoroughly comprehend and can perceive how it left an awful preference for your mouth - the video that I'd like to send you will truly help with this - it's finished by a Marketing Professor who trains network marketing at a college and somebody fruitful at it. The video isn't from our organization, it's just about the business. It truly clarifies everything in all respects unmistakably with no promotion. Give me a chance to send this to you, you watch it and after that we'll speak progressively about it."

Now and then their experience was awful on the grounds that "the organization went under" or the organization wouldn't enable them to restore the products they requested or something comparable. Subsequent to making all that they state legitimate, react with:

"I can see how that was a terrible encounter for you. Also, I'm sorry you had that experience...But pushing ahead, it's sort of like filling in as a representative for an awful organization - doesn't mean you never work again in light of the fact that you had a terrible encounter. Does that sound good to you? Or on the other hand, such as eating a terrible feast - doesn't mean you quit eating in light of an awful supper. Right?"

"Pyramid"

On the off chance that they pose the inquiry about pyramids - "Is this one of those illicit pyramids?" Answer with:

"By no means. Pyramids are unlawful. I wouldn't burn through my time or yours on something illicit. What I'm talking about is a genuine business."

(Profit to whichever venture for the Inviting Formula you were on before this inquiry). Ensure you get them to consider Brilliant to be as it improves work at completely taking care of this protest than you can without anyone else.

Okay, these MLM preparing thoughts should enable you to deal with the MLM protest. I've attempted a wide range of techniques and this one works reliably and is the unadulterated fact of the matter!

In all actuality, the MLM complaint is normal and in the event that you haven't heard it yet, keep it together in light of the fact that's will undoubtedly surface sometime. In any case, the uplifting news is, presently you're arranged and realize how to deal with these basic prospecting questions.

Utilizing the Internet to Explode Your MLM Marketing Business

Find how to detonate your MLM marketing business by using the astounding intensity of the web to make a consistent super progression of intrigued prospects who tensely need to find out about what you have doing

Envision the conceivable outcomes in the event that you saw how to gather the stunning intensity of the web to produce enough prompts fuel your MLM marketing business for a lifetime.

This isn't a fantasy or any sort of advertised up marketing gag. It's a reality for every single fruitful advertiser who have found the brilliant key that opens the entryway to enchantment city where leads stream like a relentless waterway directly into the delta of a brilliant database where upon a rainbow sparkles in support your MLM marketing achievement.

If it's not too much trouble pardon my amusing tirade however in all actuality it is essential to the achievement of your MLM marketing business and you ought to do it in the event that you need to guarantee you will have an effective MLM marketing vocation.

MLM marketing was worked for the web, it offers an approach to arrive at an intended interest group by the majority. The issue lies in the way that numerous MLM advertisers aren't using the web in a powerful way to become their MLM Marketing business.

I see this over and over:

- People sign up with a MLM marketing organization
- They register for their "organization" website whether it's free or a month to month expense is charged

- They spend huge amounts of money utilizing Google to drive prompts their MLM marketing site

This makes a major issue and here's the reason:

1. Normally the webpage your MLM marketing organization supplies is known as an "imitating" site. This is on the grounds that each and every agent inside your MLM marketing organization is being offered a similar site. The web crawlers understand this and take a gander at your website as copy webpage with non-one of a kind substance and decline to put it anyplace almost a place that would get you much wanted free traffic. Main concern, you'll be paying for guests to see your site, there's no other decision. Take a stab at structure an effective MLM marketing business, it gets costly in all respects rapidly. Trust me, I've attempted it.

2. Duplicated websites given by your MLM marketing organization are awful instruments. On account of the

inability to be special your guests won't be dazzled. Stop considering MLM marketing and have a similar outlook as a prospect for a second. What might you think in the event that you were visiting a site for the absolute first time and you saw that the individual to contact about weight reduction, wholesale fraud insurance, correspondence administrations, lawful administrations, and wellbeing and health were no different individual? Get the image?

3. Ultimately, and in particular recreated websites given by your MLM marketing organization do literally nothing to produce leads for you and your MLM marketing business. Your essential target with any MLM marketing opportunity is to create leads!

Here is a guide for what you have to realize so as to viably collect the astonishing intensity of the web and join it with your MLM marketing business.

- How to make your very own novel site (not a reproduced site given by your MLM marketing organization)
- How to adequately utilize pay-per-click search marketing to drive guests to your site (a great many people are totally ignorant regarding how to do this monetarily without spending a fortune)
- How to enhance your site for the significant web indexes (without this the web search tools won't realize you even exist)
- How to present your website to the web indexes with the goal that they are "spidered" frequently (creepy crawlies are web index robots that go all through the web searching for profitable substance)
- How to have hundreds or even a great many willing guests readily give you their contact data in return for something they need to have

- How to produce a large number of objective prompts become your MLM marketing business for FREE!!!

The way to joining MLM marketing and the web

1. Give the web search tools what they want...valuable substance (data), and
2. Give your guests what they want...valuable substance (data)

Web crawlers are intended to give their clients important data. In the event that you help the web search tools comprehend what important data you are attempting to give its clients you will be remunerated with situation of your webpage where it ends up qualified to get FREE traffic. It is by then your MLM marketing business will prosper with umber stream of consistent leads who are keen on what you bring to the table. MLM marketing and the web were made for each other. At the point when consolidated appropriately you will have a greater number of leads than you will ever realize how to manage.

Having the information about mixing MLM marketing and the web the correct way is a surefire approach to guarantee you will succeed.

Online MLM - How to Avoid Stressing Out

Stress is infectious, particularly with regards to working an online MLM business. You realize what they state around "one rotten one." Well, with regards to pressure, everything necessary is one focused on individual in the gathering to make the entire downline worried and CRAZY.

This is particularly valid for doing an online MLM business. While MLM has been around for quite a while, individuals are a few seconds ago getting their feet wet and figuring out how this business converts into the online world. Also, trust me, a ton of learning loses all sense of direction in interpretation. There are a great deal of mix-ups to be made and a lengthy, difficult experience to tool before the MLM business truly figures out how to do online marketing gainfully and effectively.

That being the situations, will undoubtedly be some worry en route. Here are only a couple of reasons for pressure.

You need to do online MLM marketing yet...

1. Nobody in your upline is doing it so you can't discover anybody to support you

2. Not exclusively is no on in your upline doing it, yet they disdain you for doing it (real pressure)

3. You can't discover instances of MLMers who are doing online MLM well AND making a decent check

4. You've composed 10,000 articles yet sold just 2 jugs of item

5. You expedite business developer's board who need to assemble online however you have no clue what you're doing, so you can't support them

6. You have been before your PC so long you're beginning to take after a PC software engineer (you know, pale white skin, red eyes, living in an eating routine of Twinkies and Coke)

7. You've been hammered so often by flamers and spammers that you're simply damn worn out...

Sound natural? All things considered, join the group. Novices to online MLM practically all offer a similar quandary. They all need to ask themselves:

"Do I have the tolerance and determination to do online MLM regardless of whether nobody else in my upline, donwline, or sideline is doing it?"

Ways to Avoid Stress in Online MLM

On the off chance that you addressed "Yes" to the inquiry above, at that point you have the "no guts, no brilliance" demeanor that it takes to do online MLM. Having said that, it should likewise be said that guts alone won't bring your business achievement while helping you maintain a strategic distance from pressure. Guts are great, yet they are only the start. To stay away from worry in online MLM, look at these straightforward thoughts:

1. Pick ONE Online MLM System to Start With

Nothing drives an online MLM novice to the insane asylum quicker than buying in to 17 distinct ways to deal with online marketing, from financed prospecting to press page craziness, and attempting to do them at the same time.

Simply STOP.

In the event that you have officially bought in to 17 distinctive online preparing frameworks, you are burning through your time as well as your money. Take a full breath, experience all of those frameworks, and pick ONE framework that impacts you. Regardless of whether you need to blog, do social media, or spotlight on article marketing, pick a framework that you really like and go with it.

In the event that you pick a framework you abhor, you'll never do it. On the off chance that you pick a framework that incorporates 300 hours of sound preparing and you are not a sound student, you'll never utilize it. Get it? Pick a framework that accommodates your character and your learning style, and guarantee yourself you will stay with it for in any event a year.

2. Try not to Spend Faster than Your Learning Curve

A great deal of online MLM preparing framework offer complimentary gift digital books, email courses, and sound exercises directly on their website. Of course, you don't "get everything" by perusing the complimentary gift materials yet these materials at any rate give you some place to begin. So before you plunk down your Visa and pay $395 for an online preparing framework "ensured" to make you rich medium-term, do the complimentary gift stuff.

On the off chance that you can't do everything proposed in the complimentary gift materials, odds are that you won't pursue the proposals in $395 program either. Besides you'll be insane focused on that you blew your home loan installment for an online MLM preparing framework that you don't utilize. Spare yourself the pressure. Try not to spend quicker than you can learn.

3. Pursue the Online Marketing Pros

When you sense that you are the just one out there doing online MLM marketing, out of touch with reality, cheer up. Try not to stretch. Rather, look at the most elite in online marketing. Look at Chris Brogan, Duct Tape Marketing, Fuel Net, Copyblogger, and even WineTwits. These folks all expertise to showcase online.

They aren't doing MLM online, however on the off chance that you can't make sense of how to adjust what they give away for nothing to your MLM business, at that point you don't merit the huge remuneration watch that you crave after. MLM represents Multi-Level Marketing. So be an advertiser. Take the best that the best bring to the table, and slice and fit their ways to deal with MLM. It's not advanced science, it's MLM. Not worth worrying over... also you can do this.

Picking Topics for Your MLM Website Or Blog

Before you begin tapping endlessly at your console and creating content for your MLM website or blog, the primary thing you have to make sense of is what you will compose.

What points would you say you are going to cover with your composing? Which questions would you say you are going to reply? What sorts of assistance and assets would you say you are going to offer individuals?

Above all, what are you going to compose that will make you stand apart from the horde of other MLM businesses marketing online?

Points for People Already in MLM

It might appear to be odd to offer tips and counsel on your MLM website or blog for individuals as of now in a MLM business, particularly if those individuals are in an alternate MLM than the one you advance. In any case, it really makes sense to help those individuals for two reasons.

Initially, by responding to inquiries with which individuals as of now in MLM are battling, you in the end become a perceived master in the field, which gives you validity and perceivability when new prospects look for a MLM business to join. Second, by offering sound exhortation that really works, you will pull in certain individuals as of now in a MLM into your business. This change rate will be little however may contribute essentially to your gathering volume.

So how might you compose supportive guidance for individuals as of now in a MLM business? Compose articles and blog entries that answer these 9 inquiries.

1. What is the most concerning issue you battle with in your very own MLM business?

2. What is the most serious issue individuals in your gathering battle with?

3. What issues are being tended to and talked about in your group or organization's preparation calls?

4. What issues are being tended to on online courses and video chats offered by different gatherings outside your group and friends?

5. What issues do you see MLMers battling with that are not being tended to by any stretch of the imagination?

6. What issues are explicit to your picked strategy for prospecting (three-

way calling, online MLM marketing, home gatherings)?

7. Where have you discovered the best answers and assets to take care of these issues?

8. What are the most widely recognized inquiries posed by MLM amateurs in online discussions or on "beginning" video chat trainings?

9. What will be the most significant issues that should be settled in MLM in the close or far future?

Reward Round

Examine a lot of individuals out there responding to questions and taking care of MLM issues. Are their answers truly working? Is it accurate to say that they are offering arrangements that really seem to be accurate to you or would they say they are simply parroting a similar old lines that you have heard in a hundred MLM courses and trainings? On the off chance that you continue hearing a similar stuff, at that point look outside the MLM business. Is there somebody in another specialty or industry who is offering arrangements that may work for MLM?

Themes to Attract People Looking for the Right MLM

The second gathering of individuals you need to compose for is the gathering searching for the privilege MLM opportunity. These individuals may not yet make certain that MLM is directly for them, yet have heard enough about the potential outcomes of MLM to be effectively doing examination. For these individuals, you need to compose content that answers addresses like these:

1. Is MLM directly for you?
2. What sort of character types exceed expectations in MLM?
3. What does it truly take to effectively do MLM as far as hours and dollars?
4. What number of various ways would somebody have the option to advertise your MLM business or item?
5. How do distinctive pay plans think about?

6. How can one examine the reputation and dependability of different MLM organizations?

7. What sort of preparing is accessible for individuals who join a MLM, and for individuals who join your group?

8. Does another information exchange need to prospect a similar way their upline does? A similar way you do?

9. What are the characteristics of a fruitful MLM business manufacturer (one who truly gains a check that covers every one of the bills, and then some)?

Reward Round

What sorts of inquiries would you be able to reply on your website or blog that will help you pre-qualify prospects before they ever dial your telephone number or zip you an email? What would you be able to inform individuals regarding your business that encourages them choose whether they need to make the following stride or not? Here are points that will help you pre-qualify leads from your website or blog:

- MLM isn't a vocation, it's a business
- MLM isn't a "pyramid scheme," ever
- MLM isn't for stiff necks yet for individuals with receptive outlooks
- Some of the best MLM business proprietors were the hardest acquire
- You will work similarly as hard at MLM as in some other independent company, yet MLM will pay you more money and for a more extended timeframe
- MLM doesn't expect you to have a lot of abilities, however having a couple of aptitudes and a great deal of readiness help you go far

Get the image?

To Attract People Not Yet Looking for MLM

This third gathering is an entire diverse pot of fish and one that I'm not going to attempt to cover in this article. In any case, when you have been composing for the initial two gatherings for some time, and have built up a special voice that individuals find fascinating, at that point you should seriously think about composition for this third gathering.

To pull in individuals who are not effectively hoping to join a MLM but rather "would be ideal for your chance," you need to embrace an entirely different style of composing. You need to compose pieces that both address this present gathering's present advantages and entice them to investigate new premiums, for example, MLM. This sort of composing is far trickier and requires much more schoolwork

The most effective method to Recruit For MLM - Top Strategies You Need To Know

How would you enroll top individuals for MLM? It is a significant inquiry and you'll certainly need to concentrate on figuring out how to enlist for MLM before you spend any money on structure quality into your MLM business.

A decent initial step for structure your enlisting prospects for your business is to find out about MLM lead age directly toward the start. It isn't unordinary to peruse advertised up tales about winding up monetarily free from a MLM business. Pictures of stupendous houses and hot fascinating vehicles are about as good anyone might expect for most new MLM organization scouts. Be that as it may, not very many people realize how to select for MLM which results in inauspiciously low quantities of effective MLM businesses generally speaking. What's more, the underlying victories will in general be fleeting.

This is definitely not a genuine marker that the MLM business model is imperfect; it just implies that a portion of the insider facts of achievement are being ignored. MLM lead age is only one of the fundamentals MLM business proprietors need to add to their toolbox.

Here are a couple of the high sway MLM business building systems and their advantages.

1. By creating lead sources you don't need to wear out your warm market of family, companions and colleagues.
2. When you're assembling a MLM downline you need to do things that can be copied by those you enroll into your business.

3. When you have starting accomplishment at enrolling for your MLM business, you can set up an automated assistant arrangement to for preparing and inspiration of your dynamic downline.

4. The leads you purchase can be worked via phone or online with your automated assistant. More is better with regards to the matter of how to enroll for MLM.

Presently how about we survey a couple of tips for boosting your MLM lead creating methodologies.

A. Most importantly, ensure the leads you purchase are moderately new. Numerous MLM lead suppliers sell drives a couple of multiple times. You'll need to necessitate that your leads are elite, which means you get them crisp and unsold.

B. When talking about crisp leads it is significant that you don't consider drives that are over 48 hours old. You need to select for MLM drives that have not been lying around holding back to be followed up.

C. Your MLM prospect leads should arrive in a bundle yet you would prefer not to purchase beyond what you can use in a sensible timeframe.

D. Top quality leads are the best. The best are the ones that give both a telephone number and email address. What's more, you'll need them qualified concerning how much the prospect can put resources into a business and how soon your prospect is accessible and prepared to begin. Main concern, the experts prescribe when you figure out how to enlist for MLM you'll need to begin first with your warm market of loved ones to make a couple of offers and get referrals.

Give me a chance to make one explanation, be that as it may, about acquired MLM lead records. I am not commonly a major devotee of purchasing leads as your essential wellspring of leads - particularly in case you're new to the business. In the event that you are going to purchase MLM leads at an early stage in your business, I would propose that you do as such exclusively to use to enable you to fabricate your telephone range of abilities. You would prefer not to burn through money on costly "new" leads right off the bat as you will wind up spending a ton of money all around rapidly.

Powerful MLM Recruiting Must Involve Multiple Steps

As you work to improve your insight about MLM selecting, don't be foolish. MLM selecting must never be a one shot presentation to your offer. Here is a generally cheap strategy that has culminated and computerized the multiple-contact way to deal with MLM enrolling.

Perusing and contemplating about MLM can persuade that MLM enrolling is tied in with structuring that one, momentous, single shot, strategy for contact that will draw all prospects into your program. It is a limited idea that is commonly bound to disappointment.

Any promoting master will reveal to you a one shot methodology is minimal superior to no approach by any means. It isn't the proposal here that on the off chance that you are doing your MLM enlisting by conveying one post card you will improve on the off chance that you send every individual on the 'hot prospect' list five post cards. It doesn't suggest that if the primary talk with a companion about MLM doesn't get him to join that you ought to bug him with five additional 'visits'. Keep in mind, most people who by one way or another end up on those for procurement, supposed, 'pick in' name and email records can't recall regularly putting themselves on such a rundown. As it were, they truly aren't keen on accepting your offer (once or multiple times) in any case.

Here is the manner by which to assemble a responsive, individual, pick in rundown of beneficiaries who are anxious to hear increasingly about MLM, and how to use it with the multiple contact approach.

First, you should ace the craft of composing short (400 to 800 word) articles on themes about MLM, which incorporate depictions of the most down to earth MLM apparatuses. (Search 'MLM article composing' or visit EzineArticles.com for its remarkable, free composition instructional exercise.) Begin by making a few dozen extremely accommodating and to the point articles. Stress themes basic for a decent fundamental MLM training, for example, MLM selecting, achievement methodologies, 'insider facts, etc.

Second, set up a blog or website on which you will post those articles. Permit free access and present it as a MLM preparing background.

Third, likewise post your web articles on a few high traffic web article destinations. There are at any rate three favorable circumstances to doing this.

1) Folks who visit those destinations read your material and become acquainted with you as a specialist and MLM master.

2) Search motors (Google and so forth) get your articles from those locales and soon you will have an overall web nearness.

3) Each article is permitted a couple of connections back to your site or exceptional offer. What's more, the majority of this is free as it directs people to your site and offer.

Fourth, on your site offer to send extra data in a bulletin or email articles. At the point when a guest 'picks in' for such a free administration you have an authentic contact, plainly keen on getting familiar with MLM and a potential enroll for your MLM program.

Fifth, (and this will cost a couple of bucks however when utilized right is well justified, despite all the trouble) set up an email automated assistant program (I contact or something like that). Each select in contact goes into the responder's mailing list. It likewise contains a few (4 to 24 or whatever you choose) incredible MLM preparing articles that are consequently conveyed at whatever interims you set - one consistently, one like clockwork, and so forth. Each article likewise contains a MLM enlisting offer on the off chance that the peruser ends up intrigued (and commonly 25% to half will in the end become intrigued. That unquestionably beats the typical 1% reaction from post cards!)

Sixth, as they go along with, they are naturally moved to the rundown that starts sending articles about MLM as it identifies with effectively working your program liberating the support from hours on the telephone giving individual clarifications.

You have taken contacts from their underlying enthusiasm for picking up something about MLM with a web search, right to ending up very much prepared individuals from your downline. You have built up your own select in contact list and contrived an approach to approach them again and again with both great preparing data and your MLM enrolling offer. The more you find out about MLM the more you will almost certainly tweak your procedure.

CHAPTER SEVEN

HOW TO PRESENT YOUR PRODUCT

Best Simple Ways to Sell your MLM Products

Is it accurate to say that you are attempting to get individuals to purchase your network marketing products? What number of individuals have you pursued to sell your MLM products just to be rejected?

It happens to us all in an independent venture. Imagine a scenario in which you could draw in individuals who really need to purchase your network marketing products.

How Attraction Marketing Works

Attraction Marketing is a strategy that draws in individuals to what you bring to the table. There is no pursuing or asking included!

OK incline toward that individuals contact you asking about your business or products?

It's much desirable over pursuing individuals down!

Consider the possibility that individuals reached you week by week or even day by day to get some information about your network marketing offer. That is actually what befallen me utilizing a basic fascination marketing recipe.

Everything begins with understanding the requirements of your group of spectators and how your products or business can support them.

Selling your MLM Product utilizing Attraction Marketing

There are numerous means to fascination marketing. I'm going to concentrate on the most significant three stages that can change your independent venture.

1 – Build an association with your group of spectators

The greatest slip-up most network advertisers make is marketing their MLM organization.

Huh? For what reason is that a misstep?

There are a great deal of different merchants marketing products from a similar organization. An individual can purchase from and get data just from doing a little look into.

For what reason would it be advisable for them to purchase from you?

It's a straightforward certainty: individuals join individuals not organizations.

Individuals like to purchase products from those they know, as and trust.

You set yourself apart by marking YOU, not your organization. Allow individuals to perceive what you are about and in the event that YOU are a solid match for them.

For instance, on the off chance that you join a MLM organization with an individual who is certifiably not a solid match for you, it can transform into a horrendous encounter.

On the off chance that an individual feels that you are the individual that can enable them to comprehend the procedure to get them where they need to be, they will go along with you.

You will be the reason that an individual purchases from you and not another merchant.

2 – Who is Your Target Audience?

Understanding your group of spectators is critical to selling your products with a fascination equation.

Before you can make a move, know the group of spectators to whom you are marketing your MLM products. It's significant provided that your group of spectators are individuals who need to shed pounds, you aren't going to market to individuals who don't have to get thinner.

Knowing precisely who your group of spectators is will enable you to make content that is important to them. The most noticeably awful thing you can do is make content that your group of spectators couldn't care less about. At that point nobody will search out your substance for utilization.

3 – What are the Challenges and Problems of your Target Audience?

What difficulties does your group of spectators face? For instance, in the event that you have a weight reduction shake, individuals who need to get thinner may get a kick out of the chance to get it? Don't you concur?

In the event that you simply inform individuals regarding the fixings, is that interfacing with their concern? NO.

The fixings are optional and don't mean a lot to the individual who is frantic to shed pounds.

Then again, on the off chance that you enlighten individuals concerning what the item does, how it can support them, and other individuals' examples of overcoming adversity, they will be progressively intrigued by your MLM item.

Presently, that you comprehend your intended interest group, you can get caught up with making content that tends to their top difficulties. Make certain to incorporate answers for their issues as YOUR MLM products!

Truly, this works. It's actually how I procured a huge number of upbeat clients.

On the off chance that you need to draw in individuals to purchase your MLM products, choose who your group of spectators is ASAP immediately. On the off chance that you don't know who precisely you are addressing, you won't probably grow a gainful business.

In the event that you are thinking about whether fascination marketing truly works, I can disclose to you that it does! I urge you to utilize the means sketched out in this post to get individuals to purchase your MLM products.

Marketing a MLM Product

In the event that you cherish selling and need to manage your very own business group, multi-level marketing (MLM) could be the road for you. Multi-level marketing is a business conveyance technique organizations use to lessen overhead costs and make expansive market reach. Organizations enroll item advertisers who sell products in return for deals commissions. Fruitful MLM agents base on making a business delegate network, just as taking part in buyer deals through gatherings or direct singular deals. The commissions got are a blend of direct deals commissions or extra commissions gotten by structure a group of marketing agents. Likewise with most deals delegates, MLM agents ought to pursue a business procedure to enable them to succeed.

1. Make a rundown of 100 individuals you know and begin reaching them about your new business. These contacts can incorporate family, companions, colleagues, neighbors or individual representatives.

2. Send an email, postcard or letter to everybody on the rundown and catch up with an individual telephone call to every individual. Tell them about your new pursuit and inquire as to whether anybody they know may be keen on hosting a get-together. Try not to hold up until you get your marketing unit from your MLM organization to inform everybody regarding your new business.

3. Host your very own gathering and welcome all your family and

companions. Request that every individual bring a companion that you don't know by and by. At the gathering, request that every participant book a gathering with you. This is an incredible method to book future gatherings from the beginning. Regardless of whether you don't book parties from the occasion, get contact data for visitors you don't know for follow up sometime in the not too distant future.

4. Make a social networking site for yourself and your new business. Utilize more than one network to extend the compass of your MLM business. Through social networking, give data about your products, the business and related data that is helpful to your supporters. On the off chance that your MLM organization is offering exceptional arrangements, update your site with the idea as quickly as time permits.

5. Begin a month to month e-pamphlet to enlighten individuals concerning uncommon arrangements, and give

accommodating and applicable data about your item territory. Utilize the bulletin to build up yourself as a specialist in the item region.

6. Join business networking and social gatherings to make new contacts and get referrals. Individual contact is another association with potential clients, either through deals to bunch individuals or referrals assembled from your connections. Offer your item data and impart your insight to other people.

7. Begin early and make energy for your marketing endeavors. In the event that your MLM organization and individual spending plan permit, buy promoting for your new pursuit.

Keys to MLM Attraction Marketing

It is safe to say that you are hoping to manufacture your MLM opportunity through MLM Attraction Marketing? In 2009 it is insightful to fuse Attraction Marketing into your business building endeavors. While we don't prescribe making it the main way to deal with structure your business it is surely a significant methodology.

Fascination Marketing as connected to MLM requires an all-around idea out marketing framework intended to get the ATTENTION of your objective market, ATTRACT them into your contact database and LEAD them to in the long run need to be in business with you. When you are building up your MLM Attraction Marketing framework then you will need to work in these 7 keys to enable you to quick follow your prosperity:

1. Comprehend Your Target Market - If you will apply the techniques of Attraction Marketing to your MLM business then the principal thing you should consider is WHO you need to ATTRACT. Numerous individuals in MLM are of the mixed up conviction that the entire world is their prospect ... you just never realize who will say yes. This conviction originates from old fashioned deduction, for example, make a rundown of EVERYONE you know and the three FOOT RULE.

Truth is the entire world isn't your objective market. The individuals who prevail in MLM ordinarily are searching for business openings or have been engaged with some type of business opportunity previously. In the event that you have perused Mike Dillard's Magnetic Sponsoring, at that point you will know his view which is the objective market is extremely other network advertisers.

When you know who you need to draw in then it is significant that get them, what really matters to them, what their torments and disappointments are, and what arrangements they are looking for?

2. Increase Exposure To Target Market - Once you know who you are attempting to ATTRACT the following stage is to create procedures to pick up presentation inside your objective market. The key here is to have the option to distinguish where your objective market assemble on mass and increase perceivability there. Today we are blessed to have social networking, social bookmarking, and other Web 2.0 apparatuses accessible.

On the off chance that you are not utilizing Facebook, Twitter, You Tube and more to pick up introduction to your objective market right now then you should end up taught on the most proficient method to do as such. In the MLM Attraction Marketing University we take you by the hand and show you well ordered through how to utilize these instruments.

3. Compelling Offer - The objective of all Attraction Marketing is to manufacture a rundown of prospects. The most straightforward approach to do this is to utilize what is known as a lead age page and make an IRRESISTIBLE OFFER. So the inquiry you need to pose is what might be powerful to your objective market?

Well in the event that your objective market is different MLMers for example, at that point what may be overwhelming to them is data on how they can draw in more leads, support more individuals and become their MLM business. So you need to give this data to free so as to have individuals select in to your database. Intend to get a pick in pace of 25% or more.

The motivation behind why such a significant number of individuals are beginning to utilize the Freedom Duplicator framework is on the grounds that the Irresistible Offer is so solid. We give away the MLM Attraction Marketing University for nothing. Therefore our pick in rate is around 40%.

4. Include Value - Now since you have them in your database does not imply that they will pound your entryway to go along with you in business.

The inquiry you need to answer is WHY. For what reason would they need to go along with you in business? Well everything begins with relationship building. Individuals will in general join individuals in MLM businesses as an essential thought. With the end goal for you to build up the correct association with the leads you are pulling in you need to consider how you can enhance their lives. This should be possible from numerous points of view. The key is to recall that since they took up your overwhelming offer does not mean they are prepared to think about your MLM.

5. Set up Credibility - Before individuals will go along with you in your MLM they need to become acquainted with you, similar to you and trust you. You have to set up believability with them. They should consider you to be a potential accomplice in MLM who can lead them to accomplish their objectives.

So you will need to build up believability inside your developing database.

The primary key to doing this is to be in incessant contact with them. Anyway ... you don't need that contact to consistently be deals messages. You need to give profitable valuable and down to earth help to them. Probably the most effortless approaches to do this is to utilize a BLOG which you update much of the time. This will mark YOU in the brains of your database.

In the MLM Attraction Marketing University we tell you the best way to set up a blog. Actually the video preparing (which is all free) will demonstrate to you each progression you have to take.

6. Adapt Lead Generation - One of the greatest difficulties for individuals in MLM is that they rapidly become bankrupt attempting to assemble their business. Particularly on the off chance that you are building utilizing an old educational system where you are continually purchasing apparatuses to construct your business.

The upside of MLM Attraction Marketing is that as you draw in leads into your database you can change over those leads into forthright money. You do this by prescribing different products that will help them arriving at their objectives. You win a subsidiary commission from making these suggestions.

On the off chance that you have the correct framework set up, at that point you can create what is known as a self-financed lead age framework where you move from having leads cost you money to you really making money on lead age. When you can turn a benefit on your lead age exercises you can pull in all the MLM drives you need without it costing you money. This implies there is no restriction to how huge you can develop your lead age framework.

7. Development - Following up with your leads will represent the moment of truth your achievement in MLM. One of the extraordinary fantasies of Attraction Marketing for MLM is that the framework will do it just for you including supporting individuals into your group. Newsflash for you ... on the off chance that you depend on a robotized framework to have individuals join, at that point your disappointment is guaranteed.

Why?

Basic ... MLM is as yet a people business. It's the connections you structure with your group that grow an effective business. So the best exhortation is to catch up the leads you have made. Call them on the telephone and state hey. Try not to attempt to sell them your chance ... simply manufacture associations with them and grow your network. In time the more individuals who know you, similar to you and trust you the more individuals will approach you over joining ... however, you should development.

In the event that you pursue these keys to MLM Attraction Marketing, at that point you can pull in more profoundly qualified MLM leads than you can deal with.

CHAPTER EIGHT

FOLLOW UP WITH YOUR PROSPECTS

What Is Follow-Up?

Follow-up involves everything that happens after the deal is shut from getting marks on all agreements and desk work to planning conveyance. It additionally incorporates your progressing association with your client. Relationship is the watchword here. In the event that you were associated with value-based selling, just centered on making the momentary deal, you would not be stressed over follow-up in light of the fact that another person in your organization would deal with it. You would proceed onward to the following client. In many retail selling situations, this might be the situation. You would not hope to get a card to say thanks from the checker at the market or the clerk at a drive-thru eatery. Be that as it may, you would hope to get notification from a realtor who sold you another home, or from a budgetary administrations advisor who is dealing with your money.

It's the scrupulousness to make certain that your exchange goes easily that you depend on your salesman to do. Consider how you feel when your salesman increases the value of your new venture with extra data and experiences. That makes you feel like a profitable client. Odds are, the point at which you need something different (another house or more money to contribute), the primary individual you will call will be the sales rep who keeps on catching up with you. When one of your companions needs to purchase a house or contribute some money, you will be in all respects prone to make a special effort to prescribe your sales rep.

Why Follow Up?

Regardless of what item you are selling, the business procedure can be testing. The selling procedure begins with prospecting and qualifying (that was six sections back!). Contingent upon the multifaceted nature and purchasing cycle of the item or administration, it could takes weeks, months, or even a very long time until you close the deal. Indeed, 81 percent of all deals occur on or after the fifth deals call

Relationship selling doesn't work that way. The relationship truly starts with the end of the deal; follow-up is the thing that causes a relationship to develop and thrive. Follow-up is the means by which most clients assess the presentation of the item or administration they just purchased. This is particularly significant when there is a hole in time between the bringing of the deal to a close and the conveyance of the item or administration (as in the conveyance of a noteworthy programming bundle, establishment of new gear, or expediting load up another item or administration merchant). A client can have misgivings, some of the time called purchaser's regret or intellectual cacophony. This is the point at which a client may imagine that the choice she made isn't the correct one. She might be in contact with a contender, get extra data, or be worried that she settled on an inappropriate choice, paid excessively, or didn't think of some as options appropriately. You can help abstain from giving your clients a chance to be defenseless against choices.

Plan Your Follow-Up

Set up together your subsequent arrangement even before you start your prospecting endeavors. While follow-up is the last advance in the selling procedure, the progression can have the most effect on your client. You endeavored to set up trust with your client during the selling procedure. After the deal is an ideal opportunity to give that trust something to do and keep on winning it consistently. Lip administration, saying that you'll accomplish something yet not so much placing in the push to do it, doesn't go extremely far in deals. Also, simply making a cursory effort will put you more distant behind. It might appear to be all the more energizing to deal with another proposition as opposed to doing catch up for a deal that has effectively shut.

Consider your subsequent arrangement in view of the accompanying five components:

1. Show your own responsibility and association with the client. Begin by saying thank you to your client for her business. Clients need to realize you care about them, their business, their difficulties, and them as people. The main reason clients quit working with an organization is a frame of mind of lack of interest. How you follow up after the deal is a decent sign of how you will react all through the relationship.

Begin on the correct foot by sending a thank-you letter. Everybody likes to feel increased in value, particularly directly after they have made a pledge to burn through money. Your letter ought to be proficient, yet close to home, and genuine. This is the ideal chance to strengthen to the client that she has settled on a shrewd choice; this is an ideal chance to emphasize the item or administration benefits with an attention on the data you found out about the client's business during the selling procedure.

Other than showing great business behavior, an individual thank-you letter likewise serves some operational goals. It ought to incorporate your contact data, telephone numbers, email address, Web locales for client contact (notwithstanding your contact data), receipt or request affirmation, and a rundown of following stages.

2. Convey as guaranteed. While you are the individual on the bleeding edge with the client, you have a group of individuals who are in charge of conveying the item or administration as determined. Set aside the effort to catch up inside to make sure all the I's are spotted and t's are crossed with the goal that your client's conveyance is faultless. That implies setting aside the effort to share subtleties and experiences about the client's business and inclinations with your whole group (regardless of whether your group is enormous or little). At the point when salesmen simply round out the structures to get things going inside, there's a high probability that a few subtleties can become lost despite a general sense of vigilance. Remember that your client made the buy since you can convey reliably for her, however you can't convey the item or administration alone. There are in all probability inward forms for correspondence and conveyance, contracts to be marked, calendars to be imparted, and other operational exercises that require the whole group to work in amicability. Pursue the inward forms and go a stage more distant. Make your colleagues care as much about conveying reliably for the client as you do; set aside the effort to share data about the client that goes well beyond your inward frames. You'll likewise be astounded to see that everybody included will include esteem association with the client. Furthermore, remember to state thank you to your group. You couldn't do it without them; share the positive input from your client with the group.

3. Enhance your client's business. Follow-up is certifiably not a one-time occasion. Or maybe, it is a progressing procedure that happens after the deal is shut. Much the same as when you looked into, posed inquiries, and tuned in to your client to learn however much as could reasonably be expected about you may settle his business challenges before he made the duty to get, you need to keep on doing likewise as a major aspect of your continuous development.

Fabricate your believability by making a deliberate follow-up framework with the goal that your client realizes he can depend on got notification from you normally. You may meet up face to face or by telephone, email, content, or a blend of these contact strategies. The key is to convey consistently in the way or habits where your client likes. It's a smart thought to get into a daily schedule to get and give announcements

Including worth goes past the run of the mill "I'm simply checking in." Every time you contact your client, offer some understanding, news, or aptitude to support him and his business. Make yourself the confided in counsel and key colleague. Give bits of knowledge from industry occasions, forward duplicates of applicable white papers, make acquaintances with topic specialists in your organization, and send organization (or your own) pamphlets. You can supplement your own catch up with the Internet to give profitable updates and networking associations through a blog, Twitter refreshes, LinkedIn dialogs, and other social networking apparatuses. Every one of these sorts of interchanges help increase the value of your client's business with the goal that when she has an issue (any issue), you convey so much esteem that she calls you first to enable her to understand it. This is the manner by which you win your seat at the table as a genuine business accomplice, not a salesman.

4. Get input. It's insufficient to converse with your clients; it's additionally critical to tune in. Request their information, knowledge, and thoughts regarding everything from things you can improve to new products and administrations. Clients, particularly those with whom you have great connections, can give important direction to you and your organization. One-on-one arranging gatherings, item improvement gatherings, and other forward-looking occasions are perfect methods for increasing firsthand input and getting purchase in from the begin. There's nothing that your client would prefer to discuss than his business. Be real and get some information about it, at that point tune in and utilize the data to support his business (and yours) develop.

5. Make your clients into fans. Concentrating on your clients' businesses as though they were yours, including worth, and demonstrating your clients that you value their business makes them more than clients—it makes them fans. Fans share accounts of their extraordinary encounters. Your clients can enable you to sell with tributes, referrals, and references. One of the best approaches to deal with protests from prospects is to approach energized and invigorated clients who are more than happy with your item and administration. There are not any more dominant words to prevail upon another prospect than those of a more-than-fulfilled client. Use client tributes as a feature of your selling introduction, on your organization's Web website, and on your expert Web webpage and social networking pages. Truth be told, it's a smart thought to approach clients to compose a suggestion for you on LinkedIn.

Top deals tips for the development

What amount of money would you say you are leaving on the business table? What number of prospects vanish without your insight regarding why? You structured an incredible marketing effort last quarter. For what reason aren't the outcomes what you needed or anticipated?

At the center, the response to the inquiries above can be summed up in one idea—development.

So often noteworthy marketing projects crash and burn in light of the fact that dimensional bundles aren't sent when guaranteed, or prospects that were lukewarm in nature become lost despite a general sense of vigilance of program organization. What's more, deals groups are famous for giving "the enormous one" a chance to get away.

A couple of straightforward advances will get those slip-ups and have you and your limited time group enjoying the good life on another arrangement of excited leads. Here are a few things you can do:

Complete Project Planning Sets You Off On the Right Track

It might appear as though an exercise in futility to put in two or three significant hours "sitting in a gathering," yet without a common vision, the advancement group can't execute an arrangement to its best potential. Deal with the gathering with clear and explicit objectives, nonetheless, and you have an abundance of potential achievement you can take advantage of. In that gathering make certain to diagram and explain the means of your crusade. Focuses to consider include:

- What the principle objectives of the battle are

- The parameters of new customer prerequisites regarding topography, size of business, where they may be in the business cycle.

- Who explicitly you need to reach (create personas just as title records)

- How you are going to arrive at your prospects as far as phone, email, postal administration, publicizing, and social media informing.

Keep in mind, it is practically difficult to catch up on a lead in the event that you have no thoughts on what your subsequent informing comprises of, both in structure and in substance.

Contact Management Systems Can't Do the Work Alone

There is a huge range of contact the executive frameworks accessible to businesses of each size nowadays. A significant number of these frameworks, when being offered to you, appear the response to every one of your needs. Item demos show you mind-bowing tips and deceives because it to appear as though you should simply download your information into the product and things will run themselves. Not really.

Human contribution, even with the most grounded devices readily available, is as yet the best value for your money. Human inclusion prompts the good judgment that product does not have, thus it is significant that when you actualize a contact the board framework, you completely put resources into preparing staff to utilize it appropriately. In the event that your deals and marketing groups don't utilize the devices you give, quite a bit of your limited time endeavors are going to fall by the wayside.

Make sure to actualize entrusting and schedule capacities with your contact the executive framework, and catch up with your group to ensure they're open to utilizing these two capacities totally. There is nothing more awful than having a customer or prospect phone you in light of the fact that their delegate hasn't got back to them after three or four solicitations.

Fundamental Common Courtesy Ensures Loyal Leads and Customers

It's stunning these days that normal affability even should be raised as an issue, yet there you have it. Individuals lose a ton of money just by getting over "immaterial contacts" or "overlooking the development" on messages left.

Remind your group week after week that individuals work with individuals they like. It's that straightforward. Saying "please" and "thank you" in a discussion is great. So is maintaining a strategic distance from the utilization of certain hostile idioms, or unfeeling language.

Encourage your group to record the guarantees they make (the utilization of an image in their gathering notes will push them the correct way), and to convey on those guarantees.

Three Follow-Up Steps Every Promotion Team Member Must Do

Our contacts are gold to our business endeavors. Perhaps the most ideal approaches to keep your contacts cheerful and drew in with your deals and marketing groups is to recognize those contacts consistently. Make sure to set enough time in your work week for these significant thank you endeavors:

1. Much obliged to you by telephone – Touch base with individuals in your database all the time, if for no other explanation than to state "a debt of gratitude is in order for working with us," or "verifying how we can serve your organization better." Then tune in. With all the social media out there, everybody's talking. On the off chance that you are the audience, you will regularly accumulate better industry news and set your business relations in this little yet profitable way to deal with business relations.

2. Much obliged to you via mail – It's valid. A manually written note has turned out to be such an irregularity, that individuals spare the thing any longer than any email or verbal affirmation. Slip your note in a splendidly shaded wrap and the administrator staff will for all intents and purposes be hurrying to ensure it goes to the perfect individual.

3. Much obliged to you by email – Okay. You have a bustling day. In the event that sending an individual transcribed note is unimaginable, in any event send a snappy email after a decent gathering. The message ought to recognize the peruser, and layout any activities from the gathering. At that point make sure to schedule those activities and development.

Restoring Prospects Who Disappear into the Black Hole

Have you at any point had hot prospects who abruptly quit restoring your call? At that point you realize how perplexing it tends to be - particularly when they'd communicated such a great amount of enthusiasm for your item or administration just days prior.

From the start, you accept their absence of responsiveness is a separated circumstance that will rapidly self-right. In any case, after rehashed bombed endeavors to interface, you begin to scrutinize your very own rational soundness.

You could have sworn they were intrigued, however their present conduct shows generally. Also, not having any desire to show up excessively edgy or to seem to be a genuine irritation, you're hindered regarding what your following stages ought to be.

Why They Disappeared

As a merchant, it's constantly critical to investigate what might cause this conduct before making a move. As far as I can tell, these are the normal reasons why prospects vanish into "The Black Hole."

- They're completely overwhelmed. Beyond question, this is the most well-known. In for all intents and purposes each organization today, individuals have an excessive amount of to do and not about sufficient opportunity to complete everything. They completely mean to proceed with the discussion, however not at this moment.

- Priorities changed. This can occur without any forethought. Changing economic situations, terrible third quarter results, and new initiative are only a couple of the conceivable main drivers. In any case, when this occurs, it's darn close difficult to recover your force for the time being.

- Lack of criticalness. In some cases merchants befuddle a prospect's advantage level with a craving to make a move today. All things considered, they share all the wonderful insights concerning their offering as opposed to building a business case for immediate change.

- Column grain. At times prospects simply need similar offers/estimating to legitimize their choice to go with another organization.

- They know it all. At the point when prospects feel they have all the data they need, there's actually no motivation to converse with you any further.

Various reasons call for various activities. Some you can avoid by doing things any other way in your client associations. Continuously be available to this probability since anticipation is your best fix. Others you have no influence over.

Regardless, you need answers! Is it "no doubt" or "nay"? It is safe to say that they are as yet intrigued or not? Would it be a good idea for you to continue pressing together them or discover new prospects?

What You Can Do

When you don't have a clue about what's behind their quiet, making sense of how to react can be an issue - particularly since you would prefer not to be an irritation. Here are a few techniques you can use in managing "The Black Hole:"

- **Just continue attempting.** Understand that prospects anticipate that you should convey the "stay in contact" load - do as well it. It can regularly take 8-10 contacts before you really contact them once more. Try not to freeze. This is typical in the present business condition.

- **Make every association important.** Don't simply say, "Howdy Eric. Simply hitting you up as I guaranteed about your xxx choice. On the off chance that you have any inquiries, call me.

- **Have a comical inclination.** After 4-5 contacts, leave a clever message, for example, "Eric. I realize you're overwhelmed. However, I likewise realize that shortening your business cycle is imperative to you. That is the reason I continue pestering you. I'm anticipating FINALLY reconnecting."

- **Leverage an assortment of mediums.** Stir up telephone calls with messages, mailings, solicitations to up and coming occasions, sending articles, and so on. To position yourself as an asset, ensures every association teaches, advises or includes bits of knowledge.

- **Create multiple passage focuses.** Never let one individual be your absolute portal to an organization. Distinguish and support multiple connections simultaneously. Whenever fitting, reference others you're conversing with in your messages/messages.

- **Re-assess your underlying association.** How might you increment their direness? Decide whether you're simply section grain? Or then again, tie your offering more into their business needs? In an excessive number of cases, dealers have done an item/administration dump when conversing with prospects. Rather you have to concentrate on basic business results and the distinction you can make.

- **Plan your subsequent stage now**. Never leave a gathering without a schoolwork task (for you and/client) and a firm follow-up arrangement booked. On the off chance that they're reluctant to do this present, it's a marker that something may not be very right - which should incite you to investigate their need and direness in more noteworthy profundity.

- **Let them free.** Send an email expressing that you thought they were intrigued, however maybe you misconstrued the circumstance since you haven't heard once again from them over the most recent a month and a half. In all honesty, this procedure regularly gets a reaction and a clarification from a prospect who is feeling remorseful about not reconnecting.

- **Reduce your contact recurrence.** In the event that, after ten contacts, despite everything you haven't heard, begin reaching them less regularly. A quarterly calendar may be progressively proper. Or then again, you should keep over what's going on in the record and reconnect at a progressively proper time.

By utilizing at least one of these methodologies, you'll frequently have the option to reconnect a prospect who has vanished into "The Black Hole." Not generally, however regularly. Furthermore, on the off chance that you've ceaselessly offered some benefit and concentrated on the effect your offering makes, they'll likely be prepared to actualize your answer yesterday.

Try not to Give Up on Follow-Up

Follow-up might be the most underestimated marketing method in presence. Independently employed experts invest a colossal measure of energy and money on pulling in or meeting individuals who may work with them. They fabricate websites, go to networking occasions, buy advertisements, set up social media profiles, and the sky is the limit from there. In any case, marketing exercises like these are planned for reaching new potential customers just because. Follow-up is absent from the image.

You've presumably heard the accompanying certainties about marketing and deals previously:

- People want to work with individuals they know and trust.
- It takes five to seven contacts with a prospect to bring a deal to a close.
- Marketing is a procedure; not an occasion.

These are for the most part various takes on a similar basic message: you should catch up with prospects, after some time, so as to get their business. Individuals who have met you or caught wind of you just once scarcely ever purchase. Be that as it may, despite the fact that the normal business visionary knows this, we much of the time overlook it when structuring our marketing approach.

The following are the five inquiries frequently posed, with certain responses to enable you to beat the snags that might keep follow-up out of your marketing.

1. For what reason would it be a good idea for me to development; won't individuals call when they need me?

No, they won't. The individual they will call is somebody they recall. On the off chance that they haven't got notification from you as of late, that individual won't be you. On the off chance that there are two proper individuals they recollect that, they will call the one they trust the most. Following up reliably after some time assembles trust.

2. Isn't catching up being excessively pushy?

Deferential, convenient follow-up isn't pushy; it's expert. When you tell prospects you will get in touch with them once more, they hope to get notification from you. At the point when prospects let you realize they are keen on your administrations, they hope to get notification from you. On the off chance that you vanish after one contact, prospects either overlook you, contemplate them, or miracle whether you are still in business.

3. How frequently would it be advisable for me to catch up with a prospect?

That relies upon how firmly you accept that prospect needs you. As a rule, on the off chance that you think a prospect's need is critical, follow up immediately, again in a few days, and again following multi week. When he/she has a need, however it isn't pressing, follow up the first run through inside a couple of days, on the other hand like clockwork. In case you don't know he/she has a need, yet the prospect accommodates your objective market, follow up the first run through inside seven days, on the other hand in any event once per quarter.

4. What would it be a good idea for me to do if a prospect never reacts?

Absence of reaction reveals to you nothing. At the point when a prospect doesn't react to calls, messages, or letters, you have no real way to know why. Keep following up on the calendar that matches what you think about the prospect's requirement for your administrations, as in #3 above. You'll be happy you did each time you arrive at a prospect on the umpteenth attempt and he/she says, "I'm so happy you called." Trust me, it will occur.

5. When would it be advisable for me to quit catching up with a prospect?

Typically, never, except if he/she requests that you stop, or you come to accept that prospect would not be a decent customer for you. An accommodating rule is to gauge the estimation of any potential deal against what follow-up is costing you. A $100 potential deal may just merit a telephone call or two in addition to a boundless number of messages. A $10,000 potential deal is likely worth numerous calls, letters, and messages, in addition to lunch.

Follow-up merits a focal spot in your marketing plan. Each marketing methodology you devise needs follow-up incorporated with it. Plan ahead of time to catch up multiple occasions with each prospect you draw in or meet. Try not to abandon development, and it will convey for you.

www.ingramcontent.com/pod-product-compliance
Lightning Source LLC
Chambersburg PA
CBHW060827220526
45466CB00003B/1004